Leisure in Society

A Network Structural Perspective

Patricia A. Stokowski

MANSELL

First published 1994 by
Mansell Publishing Limited. A Cassell Imprint.
Reprinted 1995.

Wellington House, 125 Strand, London WC2R 0BB, England
215 Park Avenue South, New York, NY 10003, USA

British Library Cataloguing-in-Publication Data
Stokowski, Patricia A.
  Leisure in Society: Network Structural
  Perspective. – (Tourism, Leisure & Recreation Series)
  I. Title   II. Series
  306.4

  ISBN 0–7201–2141–8 (Hardback)
  ISBN 0–7201–2311–9 (Paperback)

Library of Congress Cataloging-in-Publication Data
Stokowski, Patricia A.
  Leisure in society: a network structural perspective/by Patricia
  A. Stokowski.
      p.   cm. – (Tourism, leisure, and recreation series)
  Includes bibliographical references (p.   ) and index.
  ISBN 0–7201–2141–8 (Hardback)
  ISBN 0–7201–2311–9 (Paperback)
  1. Leisure – Research.   2. Leisure – Social aspects.   3. Social
networks.   I. Title.   II. Series
GV14.5.S79   1994
790'.01'35 – dc20   93–10901
                                                         CIP

Printed and bound in Great Britain by
Biddles Ltd, Guildford and King's Lynn

Tourism, Leisure and Recreation Series

Series Editors
Gareth Shaw and Allan Williams

ollege

22|10|0

Leisure in Society

Contents

Figures

Tables

Preface

Conventional wisdom in the sociology of leisure maintains that 'leisure' is a feeling of freedom and satisfaction that people experience as a result of participation in pleasurable activities during free time. Such descriptions, however, based as they are on individual perceptions, fail to capture the social character and significance of leisure behavior. Leisure is more than simply individual feelings or experience. It is a domain of institutionalized social relationships, structures, and meanings that persist across society and throughout time. Missing from our understanding of leisure is knowledge about how people construct leisure behaviors and meanings within the social contexts of their daily lives, how behaviors and meanings are socially structured and organized, and how the extended social structures of leisure subsequently exert influence on individual choices and experiences.

This volume is concerned with the social character and consequences of leisure, and specifically with one theoretical approach to the study of leisure, network structural analysis. The related topics of recreation, play, sport, and tourism are of interest because they are visible representations of leisure in society, and because they directly influence, and are influenced by, prevailing structures and meanings of leisure. Given general trends over the past decades toward decreasing work hours, early retirement, and the growth of recreation, leisure and tourist industries around the world – coupled with more recent recessionary trends, dual career or single-parent families, patterns of increasing affluence among some population segments, along with decreasing wealth for many others – one might expect that the study of leisure would hold more prominence than it currently does in academia. This volume attempts to redirect academic attention to leisure phenomena, and to reinvigorate sociological research about leisure behavior.

Today, the shift from traditional to interpretive approaches in leisure research foreshadows a more comprehensive sociology of leisure. In addition, this transition parallels current trends in all the social sciences, which are simultaneously experiencing critical reviews of taken-for-granted scientific paradigms. This volume attempts to make explicit the directions of transformation in the sociology of leisure, and to provide a preliminary structural solution for concerns about the neglect of 'context' in the analysis of leisure behavior.

This book is thus written as a response to perceived and stated deficiencies in traditional theoretical and methodological approaches in the sociology of leisure. It has three objectives: first, to review and critique the philosophical and scientific traditions that underlie sociological research in the study of leisure; second, to present a revised structural approach to the analysis of leisure, which has as its foundations the patterning of interpersonal relationships within social networks of community; and third, to illustrate applications of the approach by reviewing published research literature, discussing an example of a particular study of leisure networks, and analyzing the potential for future applications of structural research in leisure. The overall goal of this work is to provide a comprehensive introduction to the literature, and to stimulate scholarly thinking about a sociology of leisure and recreation grounded in network structural perspectives.

It is a limitation of this work that much of the reviewed literature is restricted to primarily North American sources. While leisure is becoming the subject of increasing scientific attention around the world, the distribution of analytic materials is still somewhat limited beyond national and linguistic borders. The international materials available to this American author suggest that the trends described in this volume run parallel to those in leisure research in other countries; however, specific confirmation is missing, and it should be noted that divergent orientations may exist in other advanced or developing countries.

The ideas discussed here were developed over many years during graduate studies at Michigan State University and the University of Washington, and later during academic appointments at Texas A & M University and the University of Colorado, Boulder, all in the USA. My professors, colleagues, and students at these institutions (especially Drs John Crompton, Robert Lee, and Daniel Stynes) stimulated and challenged my thinking, but should not be held responsible for any errors in judgment or scholarship I have made in writing this book. The idea for the book was conceived by Gareth Shaw and Allan Williams, geography professors at the University of Exeter, Great Britain, and editors of the critical issues series of which this volume is a part. Their generous hospitality in Exeter in July 1991 enabled me to formalize the basic outline of the book, a task made easier as a result of their stimulating intellectual company and also their expectations that I engage in some memorable leisure activities! Allan Williams also provided a careful reading of the first draft of this volume, and his insightful comments have vastly improved the substance and presentation of the final version. Editors at Mansell Publishing have been cordial and helpful throughout the writing process. Finally, and most importantly, I could not have written this book without the technical and financial assistance of the Environment and Behavior Program of the Institute of Behavioral Science, University of Colorado, Boulder, and the generous encouragement of my colleagues and friends there. Directed by economics professor Charles Howe, and populated by a select, enthusiastic set of economists, anthropologists, and geographers, 'E and B' provided a most desirable, congenial, stimulating place in which to think and write.

Acknowledgments

The author would like to thank Taylor & Francis, Inc., Washington, DC, for permission to reprint Table 1 from *Leisure Sciences* **12** (3), 251–63 ('Extending the social groups model: social network analysis in recreation research,' by P. A. Stokowski); it appears in this volume as Table 5.1. Additionally, thanks are extended to the National Recreation and Parks Association, Arlington, VA, for permission to reproduce Figure 1 from the *Journal of Leisure Research* **23** (2), 95–113 ('The influence of social network ties on recreation and leisure: an exploratory study,' by P. A. Stokowski and R. G. Lee), which appears as Figure 6.1 in this volume.

1
Leisure as an object of sociological inquiry

Those who rely on the commons enjoy a measure of control over their environment. Time and the market exert no undue pressure and work is often not clearly divided from leisure and religious activity. . . . The planting of fields or the harvesting of crops cannot be reduced to acts of production: they are also religious events, occasions for celebration, for fulfilling communal obligations, and for strengthening networks of mutual support.

(*The Ecologist*, 1992: 150–1)

Introduction

A US Peace Corps volunteer, assigned to a village in Sierra Leone, tells a story about cultural influences on the diffusion of agricultural innovations (O'Malley, 1984). In the village where the volunteer lived, it was the tradition for Sierra Leonean men to clear and plow the fields, while women planted, weeded, harvested, and stored the crops. Since harvesting and processing efforts were especially time consuming and labor intensive, the Peace Corps volunteer wanted to find a way to reduce the amount of work, and increase the amount of production, for her villagers.

During visits with the Ministry of Agriculture, the volunteer saw laborers using scythes and a new type of grain thresher to harvest and process rice. She made arrangements to introduce these technologies to her villagers, and for several days the local people tested the equipment in their own rice plots. There was much enthusiasm to try out the new thresher, and it appeared that the innovation was going to be a huge success.

However, when asked to decide whether to stay with the old methods or adopt the new harvesting and processing technologies, the villagers chose the old ways. The Peace Corps volunteer was confused: 'Why do you want to stay with the old ways, when the new methods are so much better?,' she asked. The villagers had several criticisms: ' "We can't sing when we have to bend down so far"; "We always dance and sing as we thresh the rice with sticks"; "The thresher may be fast, but it wastes time" ' (O'Malley, 1984: 27). In other words, no matter how efficient the new technologies were, they could not substitute for the communal participation and cohesion achieved through work. For these villagers, leisure and work were two sides of the same activity.

This real example from the context of international development illustrates the difficulty of defining leisure, and the mutual interdependencies of leisure and work. For the villagers, leisure was part of their daily life, indivisible from work, an intimate quality of local community life. For the Peace Corps volunteer, leisure was a commodity 'left over' from work, a segment of time that people in her culture aspired to achieve. The communal quality of leisure, as opposed to the concept of leisure as a marketable 'product' or 'service,' reflects both the nature of work and the level of dependency on local resources.

As an introduction to this book this story frames the creation and interpretation of leisure throughout history and across cultures. The nature of leisure is distinctly tied to the nature of work, the meaning of community, the enactment of social relationships, and moral and practical questions about the linkages between people and their environments. In this chapter the historical and philosophical foundations of the sociology of leisure are explored.

The Social Significance of Leisure

How is leisure socially significant? That is, how is leisure important in the real lives of people, individually and collectively? Historians, philosophers, and researchers maintain that leisure experiences have a unique character distinct from the structure and meaning of other domains of human experience, particularly 'work'; that leisure involves recreational or restorative 'activities'; that it occurs during 'free time'; and that it generates some positive emotional response or 'feeling' in participants. The various expressions of leisure known as play, sport, recreation, and tourism have been found in nearly all societies, and are important elements of people's experiences of reality.

Leisure is also big business. People spend large amounts of their discretionary incomes on outdoor recreation, sports, hobbies, travel, leisure equipment, culture, and related leisure pursuits. Complex infrastructures and organized delivery systems have evolved in order that local, regional, and national governments, and private agencies and organizations, might provide leisure and recreation services both for the enjoyment of people and for profit. Since leisure is seen as both a personal 'right' and also as a social good in many developed countries, leisure services are organized, managed, and marketed, leisure places and facilities are dedicated for public use, and leisure times, such as vacations and holidays, are regularized and institutionalized within society, so that all people may have some access to leisure opportunities.

The importance of leisure to society has been acknowledged by increasing academic attention to the phenomenon as well. Teaching programs have been developed at the undergraduate and graduate levels in universities, and research about leisure has blossomed over the past 25 years. A number of scholarly journals, including the *Journal of Leisure Research* and the more recent *Leisure Sciences* in the United States, *Leisure Studies* in Great Britain, and *Loisir et Société* in Canada, publish multidisciplinary research papers analyzing the social significance of leisure. A variety of tourism journals, notably *Tourism Management*, the *Annals of Tourism Research*, and the *Journal of Travel Research*, and several other journals devoted specifically to analyzing recreation, play, sport, and dance, also have large readerships. In addition, research about leisure and recreation appears in the disciplinary journals of geography, economics, family studies, sociology, psychology, urban planning, natural resource management, and others. Regional and national leisure research symposiums are held in many countries, and other professional meetings for social scientists interested in recreation, leisure, tourism, and park and natural resources management are held regularly in the United States and internationally.

How did leisure come to be an issue of such importance to people and societies? And what is meant specifically by the term 'leisure'? Kando (1975: 24) suggests that 'the concept of leisure is intimately related to the historical and cultural context in which it is used,' so a brief review of basic orientations to, and historic influences on, leisure provides a starting point for analyzing the roles and meanings of leisure in today's world.

Basic Philosophy and Orientation

Leisure is not a twentieth-century invention; it has been a socially significant phenomenon across most, if not all, historic periods. The meaning of leisure to a society, its role in shaping social and moral principles, its influence on patterns of social organization, and its contributions to social well-being have been topics of interest to philosophers and researchers from ancient to modern civilizations. While leisure takes forms and meanings appropriate to specific cultural and social contexts, it also retains a measure of generalizability. Evidence of this is the clustering of traditional definitions around three main topics. Leisure is commonly defined as either: (1) an 'attitude' or feeling of freedom; (2) a kind of social 'activity'; or (3) a specific 'time' period.

Leisure as 'attitude'

The classical idea of leisure as 'feeling' or 'attitude' of freedom and release from constraint reflects an emphasis on internal, personal realities, in which leisure is described as a product of subjective emotional and psychological processes (Kerr, 1962; Neulinger, 1981). Pieper (1952: 40) describes leisure as 'a mental and spiritual attitude . . . like contemplation, [it] is of a higher order than the active life.' De Grazia (1962: 233) proposes that leisure can be defined as 'an ideal, a state of being, a condition of man, which few desire and fewer achieve.' Historical records suggest that the prototypical example of this philosophy can be found in the society of the ancient Greeks.

In early Greece, leisure was conceived as an ideal, intense state of 'being' in which goodness, connectedness with the gods, and development of a contemplative spirit were of paramount importance. In Greek society, 'the treasures of the mind were the fruits of [a man's] leisure. . . . Leisure [contained] in itself all the joy and delight of life' (Huizinga, 1950: 147). Supported by a philosophy of an 'ideal man' who would strive for perfection in arts, music, discourse, sport, and military endeavors, the Greek gymnasium was the center of leisure schooling. The use of the male noun here is not trivial or inconsequential. Not all members of the society could pursue the ideal of leisure, and many of the daily workings of social organization were left to slaves, craftsmen, and women – people with far less social status than men.

The idea that only some privileged men could pursue the leisure ideal resulted from a well-defined class structure in Greek society, but also illustrated the connections between leisure and governance in the Greek states. As Hemingway (1988: 188) points out in a review of Aristotle's writing, the purpose of leisure in that society was not simply to achieve private physical and spiritual perfection, but to use one's knowledge and excellence 'for expressing virtue in political action.' Leisure was not only an individual pleasure but a public good. The leisured man was required to contribute to and improve public, communal life through the application of knowledge and virtue in politics.

In the contemporary world, the idea of leisure as an attitude or feeling generally fails to include a component of communal responsibility, but instead centers on leisure as a subjective, internal feeling of sublime experience, freedom, satisfaction, and emotion. Harper (1981) suggests that leisure is a 'lived experience' rather than a simple state of mind. Wilson (1981: 248) cautions, however, that leisure should not be considered 'an empty category of experience that is "left over" when other life-sustaining activities have been accomplished.' He proposes that leisure is central to life, a 'playful attitude . . . an alert engagement with the world.' The current term for such intense personal experiences is 'flow,' a concept used to mean the 'complete involvement of the actor with his [or her] activity' (Csikszentmihalyi, 1975: 36; see also Csikszentmihalyi, 1990). This concept is only recently beginning to receive attention from leisure psychologists (Mannell *et al.*, 1988)

Leisure as 'activity'

Another approach to the analysis of leisure is the definition of leisure as 'activity' (Dumazdier, 1967; Kaplan, 1975). In this perspective, leisure is described as '[self-determined] activity chosen primarily for its own sake' (Kelly, 1982: 23). Leisure activities are those that are freely chosen and separate from activities that obligate people to specific responsibilities, such as work tasks, or required family commitments (Kraus, 1984). In contrast to the idea that leisure can be described as an attitude or feeling, the description of leisure as activity has the advantage of objectivity: leisure activities can be counted, quantified, and compared. The principal disadvantage of such a definition, however, is that it becomes impossible to list all the activities that might potentially be called leisure, since these differ among people, places, and time periods.

An example of the definition of leisure as activity can be found in classical Roman society, which exhibited a far less idealized philosophy of leisure than the Greeks. Roman society was utilitarian, and leisure entertainments were both the rewards of urban politicians and the upper classes, as well as a mechanism for social control of the lower classes. Huizinga (1950: 174) says, 'The Roman Empire [was] a primitive community seeking to safeguard its interests by means of business relations . . . and materialistic ideals.' Leisure activities were provided as a means to maintain order in society by diverting attention away from social inequalities and '[establishing] pleasure, or freedom from pain, as the highest good' (van Ghent and Brown, 1968: 6).

The definition of leisure as activity transforms the inner reality of leisure as feeling (a psychological approach) into a reality imposed from outside (a mechanistic model). Leisure activities are seen as social objects, independent of an essentially passive subject. The description of leisure as activity frees the participant from personal responsibility to achieve a leisure ideal, and relocates the provision of leisure services to others. The model of leisure as activity can be illustrated by the development of the parks and recreation movements in modern societies. These movements were created and designed as ways to meet the social needs of people, relieve urban and work-related stresses, and formalize national sentiment about the social values of parks and leisure activities. Responsibility for some measure of the health and well-being of the public was assumed by government policy-makers and recreation service providers, rather than remaining solely the personal province of individuals.

Leisure as 'time'

The definition of leisure as 'time' refers to non-obligated or discretionary time left over after the necessary commitments of work, family, and personal maintenance are met (Brightbill, 1960; Clawson and Knetsch, 1966; Brockman and Merriam, 1973; Kraus, 1984). Time is conceived as discretionary to the extent that people can freely choose their activities. However, Rybczynski (1991) and Roberts and Chambers (1985) point out that the free choice of activities is exercised within existing cultural structures of time use, such as weekday–weekend patterns or systems of business and labor organization and social class opportunity. Discretionary time, or leisure time, according to Rybczynski (1991: 234), occurs when 'we pass . . . from the mundane, communal, increasingly impersonal, increasingly demanding, increasingly bureaucratic world of work to the reflective, private, controllable, consoling world of leisure.'

As in the model of leisure as activity, the primary advantage to thinking about leisure as a specific time period is that time is quantifiable and objective: leisure time can be measured and distinguished from obligated times in life. One of the primary research efforts associated with this perspective is that of documenting 'time budgets,' or the amount of time spent on various activities over a defined span of time (Szalai *et al.*, 1972; Robinson, 1977; Kando, 1980; Kelly, 1982). Linder (1970) extends this analysis by analyzing the influence of societal economic growth on people's amounts and uses of free time.

Inherent in this perspective is the notion of work, for without 'work' time (or time that is prescribed, obligated, and not freely chosen) there is little reason to distinguish leisure time. For example, in nonindustrial nomadic and agricultural societies, work and leisure appear to be intertwined and almost indistinguishable (Noe, 1970), and activity patterns are structured not by strict time schedules but by seasonal and environmental variations. The idea of a 'work ethic' emerged within the framework of religious and social conditions of the Middle Ages. Work was valued for its moral and economic benefits, while leisure (interpreted as 'idleness') was seen as sinful (Kando, 1975: 23). Play, recreation, and sport were appropriate for children but not adults.

The single most significant influence on the distribution of leisure in advanced societies was the Industrial Revolution. Beginning in the late 1870s, the Industrial Revolution transformed the relationships between people and nature, their gods, and each other. Kraus (1971: 169) notes that the Industrial Revolution had four major effects: (1) it created new urban societies; (2) it established an industrial life-style; (3) it strengthened the work ethic; and (4) it encouraged recreation participation during time 'left over' after work. Leisure was conceived as residual time or restorative time after work. It became the responsibility of each individual to make his or her leisure worth while.

The Industrial Revolution reinforced the separation of leisure from work, and defined progress as dependent on work and production. Industry organized life by scheduling work and its rewards, an effort that made life and nature predictable, but one that also removed some freedom of choice from individuals. The consequences of industrialization have been dramatic. Improved transportation, labor-saving devices, and communications have made life easier and basic activities less time-consuming. Life expectancy and per capita income have increased, and a new class of leisure consumers – the retired – have emerged. The number of working hours per week has been reduced, and time off for holidays and vacations is guaranteed. In the process, leisure has assumed a time and space separate from work, but is often planned, scheduled, and coordinated in the same way as work.

The definition of leisure as 'time outside work' creates several difficult logical and practical problems, however. Prime among these is the confusion in distinguishing between 'work-like' leisure and 'leisure-like' work activities. For example, do-it-yourself home projects, such as building cabinets, reconstructing basements, or painting walls, are work activities designed to raise the value of a home. But they are often done during nonwork hours, and the activities are usually not directly compensated monetarily. House-cleaning, cooking, laundry, and other activities traditionally described as 'women's work' often occur in a woman's nonemployed time, but clearly are not thought of as leisure by most women. Alternatively, some activities generally conceived as 'work' are experienced as leisure: lifeguards and ice-skating instructors find pleasure and reward in creating employment from what might be considered a hobby or a passion. Many academics, artists, and composers see their 'real work' as not teaching, selling paintings, or conducting orchestras, but as writing or thinking creatively – activities which may occur outside of typical work hours. In sum, leisure is, for at least some people, nearly indistinguishable from work. It is not uncommon to find examples of either people who 'work' at their leisure or people who lead 'leisurely' lives!

From Philosophy to Social Research

Much of the scholarly discussion about the role of leisure in society has centered around the relationship between leisure and work. Implicit in the popular and academic thinking about leisure is the notion that leisure is the antithesis of work (Wilson, 1980). Since work is generally understood to be an institutional arrangement that involves constraint of personal choice, lack of freedom, and scheduled time, leisure is assumed to represent unconstrained choice, freedom of spirit, and free time, as well as the positive emotions assumed to accompany these states. Mannell and Iso-Ahola (1985) comment that, in much of the writing about the relationship between leisure and work, leisure is conceived as a function of work. They say, 'While economic, social and political conditions in society are held responsible for the conditions of work, leisure has been seen as completely dependent on or shaped by work' (p. 156). Much of the writing about work–leisure relationships, however, operates at the level of social criticism or philosophy rather than formal theorizing.

Several authors have attempted to identify and analyze the basic dimensions of leisure (Iso-Ahola, 1980; Neulinger, 1981; Kelly, 1982; Shaw, 1985a; Samdahl, 1988, 1991). The primary dimensions of leisure identified by these authors include perceived freedom, intrinsic satisfaction, personal motivation, and low relationship to work. While research has shown these dimensions to be relatively stable across situations, it is clear that scholars have focused primarily on psychological aspects of leisure, highlighting subjective, personal qualities of the leisure experience over social qualities. Social research about leisure, in fact, may be characterized as a *social psychology* rather than a broad *sociology* of leisure.

The historical approaches to leisure as feeling, time, or activity experienced in a context separate from work, imply that leisure is socially significant, but do little to specify a research agenda about relationships between leisure and society. Presumably, the 'leisurely attitude,' or the 'leisure activity' done in 'free time,' helps keep people healthy and happy as individuals, and benefits the society as a whole. People are believed to contribute more productively to society if they experience a renewal of spirit, or revitalization and pleasure during leisure time and activities. But evidence is lacking regarding specific social mechanisms that produce these outcomes. The definitions of leisure have limited theoretical utility in social research because they fail to specify the importance and consequences of leisure within broader contexts of socio-cultural reality.

The inability of researchers to explain scientifically the *social* importance of leisure can be attributed to a number of factors, including the lack of theoretical and conceptual consistency, difficulty in generalizing across space and time, concentration of research efforts on psychological aspects of behavior, emphasis on recreation events or activities as manifestations of leisure, and a reliance on quantitative methodologies (Meyersohn, 1969; Smith, 1975). The result of such traditions is that research efforts concentrate attention on individual and small-group experiences of leisure, ignoring broader structural questions about the patterns and meanings of leisure in society. As recently as 1983, Newman (1983: 107) remarked, 'Most debate about a leisure society . . . occurs within a virtual sociological vacuum . . . factors of class, power, or wider social relationships . . . may as well not exist.'

Leisure is important to society because institutionalized processes preserve the organization, meaning, and effects of leisure across social structures. Missing from traditional approaches are propositions about the ongoing processes of social interactions and relationships that foster leisure in the context of day-to-day human experience. A complete sociology of leisure should consider the personal and collective everyday experiences of leisure and recreation in which people become involved, the structuring of leisure behaviors across society, and the meanings of these experiences for individuals and society. The major questions in a sociology of leisure should be questions of social organization: how are the relations between social actors (individuals, groups, organizations, and other corporate actors) patterned for leisure, and what do the relational patterns in this social environment mean for the behaviors and feelings of the actors involved?

These issues are important because traditional research about leisure behavior has focused on 'events' (activities) and feelings during free time, rather than on the more common 'nonevents' that occur throughout daily life.

The sociological significance of leisure, however, may be found in the regular, patterned interactions and relationships which engage people and which are satisfying and meaningful, whether they occur as special events or whether they occur simply as part of daily routine. A sociological perspective on leisure demands that attention be directed to the relationships and interactions among people that comprise leisure experience.

The Purpose of this Volume

This volume considers sociological aspects of leisure by focusing on two questions: What does leisure mean to people in the context of their daily lives? And what does leisure mean to societies in the broader organizational context of communities and institutions? These questions are related to the extent that individual behavior and choices are the visible elements of larger social structures that overlie group boundaries. Researchers must consider whether, and to what extent, leisure involves coordinated social action, and whether the consequences of such action have individual and social importance.

This volume evaluates and challenges familiar approaches and conceptualizations in an effort to develop a more firmly grounded sociology of leisure. Basic approaches to a structural sociology of leisure are described and illustrated with examples from published research literature. An alternative network structural perspective is then presented, discussed, and evaluated. It should be noted that analysis of social structural aspects of leisure is a relatively new area of research, and this volume should be considered a preliminary formalization of the subject.

Throughout this book, the term 'leisure' will be used to describe a domain of human communal experience where specific sentiments and meanings are attached to specific patterns of social relationships and behaviors. In this sense, leisure is viewed as a particular context of social reality in which social behaviors and meanings are created and objectified in day-to-day human encounters. With its focus on social structure, this definition is distinctly different from other, more traditional perspectives about leisure. Supporting evidence for this definition will become apparent as the discussion unfolds.

Unlike most analyses of leisure, this volume will not separately address issues of recreation, play, sport, or tourism – behaviors generally assumed to be related to leisure. Many scholars have analyzed these concepts in detail, and the various definitions and approaches are well documented in the literature (Huizinga, 1950; Kelly, 1982; Kraus, 1984; see also the wide range of journals in the areas of play, sport, dance, health, and therapeutic recreation). Given the orientation of this book, it will simply be assumed that all of these concepts refer to activities undertaken during, or in the context of, leisure. Since the structural propositions advanced here can be applied across all leisure activities, it is not important to distinguish between specific activity types, at least in this preliminary formalization of a structural sociology of leisure.

In the research literature, a structural basis for leisure has never been fully articulated. Thus the approach taken here is to detail the progression of ideas leading up to and supporting a structural sociology of leisure. This is a formidable task, since leisure research has grown dramatically over the past two decades, and the scope of ideas is broad. It will be impossible to review completely the entire body of published literature in both the parent discipline of sociology and the applied field of leisure research. Instead, significant writings have been chosen to illustrate ideas, and there should be no illusion that the entire body of writing is referenced.

The volume is arranged in the following manner. Chapter 2 describes traditional research approaches and findings in the sociology of leisure, and reviews the scholarly literature about small, primary groups from which leisure is assumed to derive. The contributions and limitations of traditional approaches are evaluated with respect to their usefulness in a structural sociology of leisure. In Chapter 3 more recent interpretive approaches to the study of leisure are presented. These provide a connecting link between traditional leisure research and the proposed structural approach. Components of a structural sociology of leisure are outlined in Chapter 4, and the networks approach to structural theorizing is introduced.

The history and development of the networks perspective is discussed in Chapter 5, and social networks literature potentially relevant to leisure research is reviewed. Chapter 6 presents a review and discussion of leisure research literature that applies structural theorizing using social networks approaches. This chapter also includes a brief summary of a case study illustrating the network approach to analysis of community leisure behaviors. A critique of current research about structure in leisure is presented in Chapter 7. One of the unresolved problems that accompanies this approach is understanding 'meaning' in the leisure experience. The structural approach implies a social, not individual, solution to the problem of meaning, and possible resolutions are presented in Chapter 7. Finally, in Chapter 8, the consequences of a structural sociology of leisure are examined.

2
Traditional approaches in the sociology of leisure

The great discovery of the ancient world (about 600 B.C.) was that there was an intelligible structure to the world. The great discovery of the Renaissance in Europe was that we could use this structure for our purposes, that the more we understood it, the more we could control matter and energy. The great discovery of the present-day revolution is that, within limits, the structure is up to us, and different formulations of it must be used with different types of experience and to attain different goals.

(Le Shan and Margenau, 1982: 28)

Introduction

What has the sociology of leisure been, and what should it become? The sociology of leisure is a subset of the discipline of sociology which applies sociological reasoning, theories, and methods to leisure phenomena. Disciplinary boundaries, and the scope and focus of research efforts in the sociology of leisure, have traditionally been wide and varied, reflecting the breadth of philosophies and theoretical orientations in the parent discipline. Parry (1983) notes that a number of sociological traditions have informed leisure research, including: industrial sociology; studies of community life; analyses of social class and status; social welfare research and analyses of deviant behavior; research about the effects of the life cycle on leisure; and research about mass culture and subcultures. While a complete review of all the literature on each of these topics is beyond the scope of this volume, this chapter presents a brief discussion of some of the most important concepts and ideas analyzed by leisure sociologists, and then reviews general theoretical approaches in the sociology of leisure. As noted earlier, much of the literature discussed here is drawn from North American sources; it is acknowledged that the selection of this set fails to reflect adequately the substantial contributions made by scholars elsewhere.

Sociological Reasoning

The fundamental question engaging sociologists is, 'How and why is society possible?' (Turner, 1982). Individuals live in a social world, in the company of many others, and the study of sociology centers on analyses of the processes by which people collectively create, maintain, and transform patterns of order and organization to provide meaning for their experiences. Sociologists study the relationships between individuals and society by analyzing *'social trans-actions'* of all kinds . . . joint enterprises involving the coordinated efforts of two or more participants' (emphasis in original) (Shibutani, 1986: 5). Social transactions include both formal and informal social interactions which collectively shape the fabric and structures of society.

The fundamental assumption of sociology is that society is not a random, inconsequential practice, but is the result of relatively predictable patterns of social relationships and interactions among people. Given such an assumption, scholars and researchers employ scientific procedures to uncover the patterns that constitute society. These analyses proceed on a variety of social levels (micro to macro) and draw from a variety of theories about social behavior (functionalism, conflict theory, and symbolic interactionism, to name only a few).

The application of theories is influenced by prevailing philosophies about 'how the world works.' That is, the notion of 'reality' differs across theoretical perspectives. For example, a mechanistic model of reality conceives of the world as an orderly, machine-like system which has an independent order. Smith (1979: 4) comments, however, that '[human] intentions, meanings, values, and beliefs . . . are not "real" in a mechanical world.' Functional theories are often criticized for being too mechanical, or for relying on solutions that give primacy to a stable, orderly world. An alternative to mechanism is the 'intentional model' of social behavior, in which an actor is seen as purposive and as having some control over the 'creation' of reality. Under an intentional model, society is created and re-created through the ongoing processes of human social interaction. Symbolic interactionism and phenomenology are two theoretical perspectives that adopt intentional perspectives.

Sociological theorizing, in sum, is concerned not only with individual behavior and action but also with the relationships of individuals to society. While this idea may seem self-evident, this book adopts the position that the point has not been taken seriously enough in leisure research. As it appears today, the sociology of leisure may be better described as a social psychology of leisure, focusing primarily on individual experiences, rather than on social contexts and structures of leisure.

Traditions in the Sociology of Leisure

What are the intellectual traditions that have guided sociological thinking and research about leisure behavior? There are at least three discernible intellectual periods in the history of the sociology of leisure, including: (1) a formalization period, in which ideas and boundaries of the topic were outlined; (2) a period of empirical research dedicated to establishing a body of basic and applied results; and (3) a more recent critique of traditional approaches. To some extent, these trends have bloomed and faded in response to societal and disciplinary influences, and they appear as general rather than discrete time periods. The first two trends (theory formalization and applied research illustrations) are discussed in Chapters 1 and 2, while the third (the critique of traditional approaches) is discussed in Chapter 3. These reviews are intended to illustrate how a structural sociology of leisure might derive from and also build upon existing research traditions.

Theoretical formalization

The study of leisure was not considered an independent discipline until after World War II but, prior to that time, many significant sociological writings had included some analyses of leisure behavior. These took the form of analyses of the fabric of community life, and research about economic development across society. Several important writings focused specifically on analyses of leisure in social or economic terms, including Veblen's (1899) economic analysis of the 'leisure class,' and Lundberg *et al.*'s (1934) analysis of leisure in the context of suburban life. Other authors incorporated analyses of leisure into broader research about community life: for example, Lynd and Lynd (1929, 1937) analyzed social behavior in the community of 'Middletown,' and, later, Komarovsky (1962) studied leisure as one component of the marriages of working-class adults. Parry (1983), reviewing the development of the sociology of leisure in Britain, documents similar trends in research topics.

The basic theoretical foundations of a sociology based on relational aspects of leisure were articulated primarily between 1955 and 1975. Increased levels of affluence, growing amounts of free time, and the creation of 'mass leisure' and leisure 'consumers' through advances in technology (symbolized initially by the popularity of television), resulted in concerns about the 'problem of leisure.' In response, sociologists attempted to identify the critical issues and boundaries of the new relational sociology of leisure by acknowledging 'the importance of social interaction either as leisure activity itself or as part of other activities' (Crandall, 1979: 170).

Work and leisure revisited

In one of the earliest evaluations of the sociology of leisure, Berger (1962: 37) noted that 'The sociology of leisure today is little else than a reporting of survey data on what selected samples of individuals do with the time in which they are not working and the correlation of these data with conventional demographic variables.' He proposed as an alternative that the sociology of leisure should be concerned with 'the moral character of a style of life [expressed in] the behavior of groups under conditions where that behavior is least constrained by exclusively instrumental conditions' (p. 45).

Berger made the distinction between instrumental relations of the workplace and the less binding, informal social relations which seemed to govern the domain of leisure. He maintained that leisure was not neutral, but was a moral context inextricably bound to meanings of work in culture. Though he did not elaborate on the linkages between leisure behavior and social group contexts, his paper provided the ingredients for later conceptualizations of leisure as a product of primary group involvement.

The relationship between work and leisure, and the functions of social groups in leisure, was further addressed by Cheek (1971). He studied the social organization of work and 'not-work' (i.e., leisure) contexts of life, and found that people usually participated in work activities as individual 'social persons,' but participated in not-work activities as members of 'social groups.' Further, he proposed that leisure settings differed from work settings in that they required activities that 'build interindividual identification (such as gestures of appreciation) and generate intergroup solidarity (such as sharing of social goods)' (p. 251). Cheek suggested that the differences in social organization between work and leisure might provide the basis for a theory of leisure behavior.

Outdoor recreation settings

In addition to these general theoretical statements about relationships between work and leisure, the setting of outdoor recreation presented an opportunity for further detailing the boundaries of a new sociology of leisure. In the United States, the establishment of the Outdoor Recreation Resources Review Commission in 1958 brought together leading social scientists to study patterns of leisure and recreation participation in various outdoor settings. The efforts of these eminent social scientists produced 30 pioneering reports by 1962; the reports were generally viewed as marking the beginnings of formal interest in the study of leisure by scholars across a variety of disciplines (Burdge, 1983).

The importance of leisure settings for social interaction was described in ORRRC Report No. 20 (Mueller and Gurin, 1962). Analyzing findings of a national survey of recreation participation, the authors proposed that outdoor recreation settings offered opportunities for people to engage in activities with significant others in their lives. The authors noted that 'Often [people] said they became interested in [an] activity because it was something they wanted to do with their spouse and children' (*ibid*.: 37). Social considerations of recreation participation were discussed in more detail in ORRRC Report Number 22 (Frank *et al.*, 1962). These authors hypothesized that:

> The social frameworks within which people conduct their outdoor recreation activities have . . . unique role assignments, status relationships, achievement norms, and so on. These special social structures are major links relating individuals to recreation resources, hence making it difficult to describe either users or resources, except as they are defined within the social context. (p. 247)

Their statement is notable for the emphasis it places on the functions of group membership in recreation and other free-time pursuits, and on the importance of social structures in mediating between people and resources. These two issues continued to take precedence in most of the sociological analyses of leisure over the next two decades, as the legacy of the ORRRC reports influenced subsequent research efforts. The focus on social groups emphasized the arrangements among sets of people at leisure and recreation places, and raised questions about the influence of group membership for behaviors. Appropriate issues for study included roles, social norms, reference-group effects, group cohesion, life cycle influences on groups, and individual psychological characteristics related to group membership.

Leisure in extended relationships
The focus on primary social groups (and the accompanying social-psychological theorizing) guided much of the sociological research about leisure for several decades. In contrast, one of the most interesting elaborations of sociological theory was presented by Burch (1969), who proposed a 'personal community' hypothesis as the basis for leisure and recreation behavior. He suggested that people lived in relatively stable 'personal communities' containing multiple 'circles' of immediate and extended family, friends, and colleagues. Within different circles, people shared interests and activities, and individuals were socialized into recreation styles. Hypothesizing that people were likely to choose specific recreation activities and styles because they were socialized into leisure patterns through relationships with others in their social circles, Burch suggested that 'The nature of the intimate social circles which surround the individual may be the crucial determinant of variation in leisure behavior' (*ibid*.: 125).

Burch's ideas, published even prior to much of the writing about social groups in leisure, anticipated research about the role of leisure in the daily lives of people. His work provided a foundation for considering leisure across the life cycle, leisure socialization processes, and the social contexts of leisure expressed during day-to-day experiences. His classic article implies the necessity of locating social groups within broader structures of society, and locating leisure within the activities of daily life. His work redirected the research focus in the sociology of leisure away from the onsite aggregate called a social group and toward the broader influence of sets of family and friends outside recreation events. In addition, even though his theorizing remained centered on individuals, his writing provides a starting point for theorizing about the structural consequences of social circles. By linking individual and personal community ideas, his work provides a unique contribution to leisure research.

Summary

The theoretical approaches outlined and adopted by leisure scholars defined the scope of research issues and the kinds of questions that later guided the study of leisure behaviors. Leisure, initially viewed under the sociological perspective of functionalism, was contrasted with work and evaluated for its potential to contribute meaningfully to individual and social well-being. Later, researchers using interactionist perspectives provided new research agendas centering mainly around social interactions within small, primary groups consisting of family and friends. From the interactionist perspective, the important questions about leisure behavior were questions about the composition of leisure groupings, the enactment of individual roles within the context of group membership, and the processes by which groups facilitated and legitimized members' social actions and meanings about leisure. Groups were conceived as mediating influences between individuals and leisure experiences.

Table 2.1 illustrates the development of three intellectual traditions in the sociology of leisure. Critical issues addressed during each time period are outlined and, while the periods are not mutually exclusive, each produced and extended significant theoretical and empirical issues. Table 2.1 provides a reference guide for the issues discussed in Chapters 1–3 of this volume. In the remainder of this chapter, and in Chapter 3, a sampling of empirical studies will be presented to illustrate traditional and interactionist theoretical perspectives in leisure research.

Empirical research: illustrating the theory

The theoretical issues raised by leisure sociologists directed subsequent research efforts about the role of leisure in the lives of individuals and across society. Over the past few decades, several trends in research applications have become evident. Researchers initially focused on obtaining basic descriptive information about leisure participation by surveying individuals at recreation places and aggregating data about personal and social characteristics. The purpose of such research was to document the growth of leisure and recreation in society, and to examine potential causes and effects of increasing participation in leisure and recreation activities by people in different social circumstances.

Later, researchers attempted to predict leisure participation by analyzing the social contexts in which activities occurred. These studies centered primarily on the influence of social group membership on individuals, and much of the research was conducted in outdoor recreation settings. Peaking in the 1970s,

Table 2.1 Development of the sociology of leisure

Three periods	Disciplinary issues and topics of research interest
1. Formalization period (Chapters 1–2)	1. Philosophical dimensions: leisure as attitude, activity, and time 2. Leisure as the antithesis of work 3. Analysis of socioeconomic conditions, leisure as 'social problem,' dimensions of leisure, cultural framework of leisure 4. Individual level of analysis; social aggregates across society
2. Empirical leisure research (Chapter 2)	1. Descriptive analysis of recreation participant characteristics, aggregated across recreation activities 2. Analysis of primary social groups during onsite recreation 3. Analysis of leisure in family groups over life cycle 4. Theorizing about 'personal communities' in leisure 5. Social analysis of outdoor recreation settings and meanings, tourist experiences and places
3. Critical and interpretive approaches (Chapter 3)	1. Critiques of traditional approaches to leisure research 2. Development of interpretive sociologies of leisure: symbolic interactionism, phenomenology, exchange theory 3. Analyses of leisure contexts and leisure meanings: common leisure occasions, voluntary associations, social worlds of leisure, extended relational ties

these studies were partly fostered by an increased use of public lands for recreation purposes, and an increased understanding of the importance of social aspects of natural resource management. In the United States, many of these studies were supported by federal agencies such as the National Park Service and the US Forest Service, in an effort to derive policy for public lands management. Following closely behind this research agenda was an emerging interest in the role of leisure in the daily lives of people, across all stages of the life cycle. As the 'baby boomers' generation reached middle age in the 1980s, much of the research about leisure came to be centered around issues related to the roles and meanings of leisure throughout the life course.

In the following sections, illustrations of these empirical contributions to the sociology of leisure are presented. The discussion focuses on the three topics identified above: basic research about social characteristics; research about social groups in outdoor recreation; and analyses of family life cycle issues. Since the literature on these topics is extensive, only selected writings are presented.

Basic description
The earliest efforts to study leisure behavior focused on describing the settings, activities, and time periods of leisure, and also on recording the segments of

people who engaged in various kinds of activities. This research attempted to stratify visitors to recreation places on the basis of their personal and social characteristics, such as age, sex, education, race, income, and occupation. The goal was to document and predict leisure participation patterns as a function of social class and status.

National and state recreation planning studies, including some of the ORRRC reports (1962), economic analyses of recreation demand (Clawson and Knetsch, 1966), and other studies of activity participation (for example, Clarke, 1956; Burdge, 1969), provide examples of this type of research. Many of the findings are self-evident: for example, lower-income individuals do not participate in downhill skiing or take cruises to the extent that higher-income individuals do; older people participate in backpacking and rock climbing less frequently than younger people; and parks are likely to have different meanings for working-class and upper-class visitors who use those recreation settings for different activity purposes.

The question of how social class influences leisure has long been debated. The concept of 'class' differences refers to the stratification of members of a society by such measures as economic level and occupation. One of the earliest commentaries about this subject was Veblen's (1899) theory that leisure was a means of ensuring social status and maintaining class distinctions between people and groups. He suggested that, in both historical and contemporary situations, the wealthy 'possessed' leisure, participated in leisure through conspicuous consumption, and used leisure to exclude lower-class members. Veblen's theory reflects the vertical structuring of class relations across societies. Horizontal relations are also important: even within classes, the patterning of work time influences leisure opportunity. Roberts and Chambers (1985) report that abnormal work shifts and schedules differentially affect working-class women and ethnic minorities, who experience highly reduced leisure activity participation. The combination of work-time requirements and other structural constraints (social segregation of minorities, or family and household demands on women's free time), results in racial, ethnic, and gender inequalities within social classes.

A recent review of literature about relationships between social class and leisure participation was presented by Dawson (1988). He documents two related themes that characterize many critical analyses of the function of leisure in capitalist society. The first theme, that leisure 'reproduces' the social organization of labor by reinforcing capitalist rationality and class inequalities, is demonstrated by the institutionalization of middle-class values in play and sport, and the status restrictions of such leisure places as parks. This theme is countered by an opposing view which holds that leisure provides 'a site of resistance against capitalist cultural forms' (*ibid.*: 193) through the development of relatively separate, autonomous leisure subcultures, such as that illustrated by a working-class saloon.

Much of the basic descriptive research about leisure behavior includes analysis of social stratification variables in combination with indicators of psychological states such as personal motivations, arousal levels, satisfaction, and sense of freedom. The most comprehensive presentation of the social-psychological approach to the study of leisure is Iso-Ahola's (1980) text, *The Social Psychology of Leisure and Recreation*. More recent research about sociopsychological elements of leisure includes work on ego involvement and attachments to leisure (Selin and Howard, 1988), analysis of leisure boredom (Iso-Ahola and Weissinger, 1990), the study of moods produced by leisure (Hull, 1990), and research about leisure constraints (Jackson, 1991) and leisure involvement (Havitz and Dimanche, 1990). Class and status variables are used both to explain and to predict modifications in the psychological variables under study.

While there is a wealth of basic descriptive research about leisure, many of the findings are inconclusive regarding the effects of variables on patterns of leisure participation. Recent work by Murdock *et al.* (1991), using population trend data to project participation patterns in outdoor recreation activities, illustrates the uses of such data. The authors suggest that as the population ages, growth rates slow, and as the proportion of minorities increases in the United States, rates of increase in outdoor recreation activities will slow as well. There is a need for cross-cultural research on these and other related topics.

The study of basic characteristics of populations assumes that subgroups of people will continue to participate in leisure in a generally stable manner. That is, a large proportion will continue to take driving trips for pleasure, another segment will continue to golf, yet another subset will have the demographic and socioeconomic circumstances to become involved in figure skating. West (1982, 1984) challenges this view with his analyses of 'status-based diffusion' processes. He proposes that diffusion of rapidly growing recreation fads is a nonrandom process stimulated by mass media and advertising, influence from high-status strata (high education, high income) to lower strata, and status-seeking behavior. In testing the model, West (1984: 350) found that 'social influence occurs primarily within the same or closely adjacent status groups, and that influencers tend to have the same or slightly higher status than adopters.'

Researchers have recently begun systematically to study social and economic variables that are assumed to produce differences in leisure participation and behavior. One issue that has received increased attention is racial and ethnic variation in leisure activity participation (Cheek *et al.*, 1976; Woodard, 1988; Irwin *et al.*, 1990). Hutchison (1988) suggests that the lack of cumulative results about the influence of race and ethnicity on leisure stems from several problems, among them 'a failure to adequately define and operationalize the theoretical constructs of "race" and "ethnicity"' (p. 10). Allison (1988: 253) notes that the 'dynamics of racial [and] ethnic differentiation and expression' are muted in traditional aggregation techniques common to survey research. She suggests that interpretive, qualitative research approaches and contextual analyses may help distinguish meaningful features of leisure behavior across ethnic boundaries.

Social groups in outdoor recreation

Standard socioeconomic variables tend to be relatively poor predictors of the frequency and nature of outdoor recreation participation. However, when a social group variable (such as participation with family, friends, or mixed groups) is included with the socioeconomic analyses, 'the amount of variance explained with regard to frequency of participation in a specific activity increases significantly' (Field and O'Leary, 1973: 23). Interest in social group characteristics grew from repeated observations that people tend to visit recreation places primarily with others, rather than alone, and that 'the others usually constitute a recognizable social group' (Burdge *et al.*, 1981: 5).

The first published research about social groups appeared in writings about leisure and recreation in the 1962 reports of the Outdoor Recreation Resources Review Commission. In studying the satisfactions people experienced from visiting parks, the authors of ORRRC Report No. 5 (Department of Resource Development, Michigan State University, 1962) analyzed the group formations of recreationists at 20 park and forest areas across the United States. In this study, the authors defined the term 'user group' to include the following: (1) single families with or without children; (2) two or more families together; (3) a family plus friends and relatives; (4) a group of friends; (5) an organized group such as a team, troop, or club; and (6) one person alone. These group types provided a formal taxonomy adopted in many of the studies that followed.

The ORRRC writings set the stage for further definition and refinement of the social groups model in recreation research. One of the first published studies to confirm the importance of social groups at recreation places was Etzkorn's (1964) analysis of the social aspects of camping. While attempting to determine the recreational values that campers placed on their experience, the author was surprised to find that 'More startling than the [socioeconomic] regularities would seem to be the tendency among the studied campers . . . to derive major satisfactions from the social resources of the social system of the camp' (p. 78).

Etzkorn found that camping at public campgrounds was primarily an activity done by family groups, and suggested that campers were attracted to the activity because 'the social relationships of the camp provide . . . opportunities to maximize satisfactions from (similar) social interests among the campers' (*ibid.*: 86). Etzkorn's systems view provided a rationale for the link between social interaction and recreation satisfactions, and also raised an important issue that was not addressed until much later by researchers: the distinction between 'within group' and 'between group' interactions at leisure places.

That is, while the social group with whom one goes to a recreation place has its own sets of relational connections, the opportunity for interactions with other visitor groups onsite creates possibilities for the formation of new sets of communal relationships and interactions. Relational ties both within and external to the primary group represent potential influences on the success of the recreation experience.

The potential of the social groups model seemed apparent in the early and mid-1970s when many researchers incorporated social group variables and interactionist theorizing in their studies. Burdge and Field (1972), reviewing empirical approaches in the study of outdoor recreation, encouraged the use of social group variables. Cheek (1976), studying visitors to zoological parks, reported that 96 percent of adults sampled visited zoos with other people, and 'the social groups with which they had gone were comprised of relatives, friends, and occasionally a neighbor, with very few groups including people from their work, clubs, or sporting groups' (p. 54). Moreover, he noted that visitors tended not to interact with other visitors outside their immediate social groups at the zoo.

Field and O'Leary (1973) combined social group variables with socio-economic and demographic variables in an effort to describe participation patterns in water-based recreation activities such as swimming, fishing, power boating, and visiting a beach. Field and Cheek (1974, 1981; see also Cheek and Field, 1977) studied the relationship between water-based activities and specific natural resource areas and found that different social groups and individuals enacted a variety of activities at leisure settings. Some visitors came to water-based areas to fish, others to picnic, socialize, or to play games. On the basis of their findings, the researchers suggested that 'Resource [places] cannot be distinguished by the recreation activities occurring on them' (Cheek and Field, 1977: 67).

If activities do not distinguish recreation places, then either the setting itself or the social groups who visit may be responsible for variation in recreation behaviors and meanings attributed to the experience (Cheek *et al.*, 1976). The specific qualities of leisure settings that could affect both activity participation patterns and social group composition have been the subject of a number of research studies (Bultena and Klessig, 1969; Lucas, 1970; Knopp, 1972; Cheek and Burch, 1976; Lee, 1977; McCool, 1978; Baumgartner and Heberlein, 1981). Lee (1972) suggested that meanings attributed to the recreation experience are socially created by groups who use leisure places for different purposes. Because meanings are created socially, they become objectified by recreation participants and incorporated into recreation subcultures. He proposed that 'Outdoor recreational settings might best be understood in terms of the meanings assigned to them by particular sociocultural groups' (p. 68). Buchanan *et al.* (1981), reviewing the literature about social groups as centers of meanings within recreation activities, agreed with Lee that 'the source of different meanings [within an activity] is different social groups' (p. 256).

Several evaluative papers have attempted to judge how well the social groups model has served leisure and recreation research over the past quarter-century. Christensen (1980) reanalyzed Field and O'Leary's (1973) combination of social group plus social aggregate variables in studies of water-based recreation activities. He demonstrated that a confounding of variables occurs at the point of intersection between a social group variable (for example, participation in a fishing group) and a social aggregate variable (for example, age). He notes that

> It is not possible to determine the expected change in the level of participation in fishing for a unit change in age . . . because it is not known if the change in age also brings about changes in the social group in which one participates in fishing. (p. 350)

Christensen concluded that a social group variable is useless unless researchers specify theoretically the points of intersection where social group and social aggregate variables might interact with one another.

In another critical analysis of the social groups model, Dottavio *et al.* (1980) compared the predictive power of socioeconomic variables and social group variables in explaining two aspects of a dependent variable (frequency of recreation participation, and high/low participation). Using data from a statewide outdoor recreation demand study, they found that

> The social group was a more effective explanatory variable of participation in outdoor recreation activities than were socioeconomic/demographic variables. . . . [However] when the dependent variable was specified as high or low participation . . . the effect of the social group decreased and the effect of socioeconomic/demographic variables increased. (p. 364)

The authors attribute the changing contributions of each independent variable to the level of precision in specification of the dependent variable ('frequency' is recorded as an increasing numerical count; 'high/low participation' is a dichotomy). The conclusion reached by these authors and by Christensen is that specification of key variables relative to social groups is a necessary step for achieving both theoretical and practical progress in recreation research.

The use of social group variables in leisure research was originally seen as a way to categorize users of recreation and leisure places. Once social theorists found that groups seemed to be the prevalent form of leisure participation, their attention turned to analyzing the functions and processes of primary group interaction. Sociopsychological theories of small-group behavior were employed in the study of leisure identities, activity preferences, social constraints and benefits of leisure, and other applied issues, such as analyses of encounter norms in outdoor settings (see, for example, Shelby, 1981; Noe, 1992). These issues are discussed in more detail by Manning (1986), who summarized the history and applications of the social groups model in leisure and recreation research.

Applications of the social groups model also developed in studies of tourism behavior. Crompton (1981: 563) found that social groups among pleasure travelers '[facilitated] a satisfying vacation experience [by] saving money, ameliorating loneliness, stimulating additional perspective, and providing a sympathetic forum for recalling and reminiscing about vacation experiences.' The social groups model has also been implicit in analyses of tourist roles, social and cultural impacts of tourism, host–guest interactions, and other ethnographic tourism research. For example, travel groups mediate between individual tourist encounters with strangers (Greenblat and Gagnon, 1983), and travel partners experience 'heightened excitement in sharing' that reinforces the 'sacred charisma' of the touristic activity (Graburn, 1989: 34).

The tourism literature also suggests that residential groups in destination communities differentially experience impacts when mass tourism ensues. McGoodwin (1986) and Greenwood (1989) document cultural disturbances related to the 'commoditization' of local folklore and festivals, and report increasing disorganization of social relationships between groups of residents. On a more abstract level, MacCannell (1976) provides a speculative treatment of tourist relations, viewed from the perspective of both individuals and tourist groups who 'consume' experiences, and destinations that 'produce' tourist experiences. His structural ethnography of the 'ritual performances' tourists create while sightseeing, and the 'staged authenticity' provided through tourist attractions, develops from consideration of the social relations that comprise Western society and are reproduced in the context of tourism. His work suggests further possibilities for research about social group influences on the creation of tourism meanings, a topic also of interest in the literature about host–guest interactions (Smith, 1989).

Among leisure researchers, the social groups model maintained popularity throughout the decades of the 1970s and 1980s, illustrating the elaboration of interaction theories in leisure behavior. The social groups model set the stage for theorizing about interactions and relationships within groups, a direction that was further expanded in research about leisure in family settings and throughout the life cycle.

Family leisure: life cycle concepts
While much of the social groups literature in recreation and leisure developed around studies of visitors onsite at leisure and recreation places, another research theme has evolved around the study of leisure contexts across life stages. This research can be seen as a theoretical extension of the 'social circles hypothesis' proposed by Burch since it emphasizes the influence of sets of others, primarily family and friends, on leisure choices and participation. The sociometric and interactionist approaches utilized in this research have produced theoretical and methodological innovations that increase understanding of leisure roles, dyadic and small-group interactions, family influences on leisure, leisure participation throughout life, socialization through leisure, childhood development for recreation and leisure, and aging. Orthner and

Mancini (1990) review the development of research about family bonding and leisure, and propose topics for future research.

The concept of 'family life cycle' provided an orientation for researchers attempting to predict leisure behaviors for people of different social circumstances. As applied in research, the concept refers to 'significant changes in leisure [that] are related to work, changing resources, opportunities, role expectations, and self-definitions through [the] age-related sequence' (Kelly, 1983: 54), from childhood and youth through married adult and aged years. The importance of the family setting for learning recreation activities, and the influence of family and friends on leisure socialization, has been studied by Kelly (1974, 1978), and Yoesting and Christensen (1978).

Primary groups, such as the family, are important for the initiation of future social roles. The structuring of work in relation to family and leisure time was explored by Hantrais *et al.* (1984). Horna (1989) discussed the role of leisure in defining and enacting the parental role. Scott and Willits (1989) found positive relationships, especially for women, between adolescent and adult leisure participation patterns. In studies of family recreation participation, Kelly (1978: 47) concluded that 'leisure associations and orientations change during family life cycles . . . [but] family interaction is seen as a most important component' for achieving satisfaction in recreation activities.

An early study of social interaction in the family group as a whole was West and Merriam's (1970) analysis of the effects of recreational camping for sustaining and increasing 'family cohesiveness.' Cohesiveness was measured as the amount of intimate communication in the family social group. The authors found that 'early stages in the family life cycle are associated with greater family outdoor activity and higher scores on family cohesiveness' (p. 256). That is, younger families report more cohesiveness and greater levels of participation together in outdoor recreation.

In a survey of Iowa households, Christensen and Yoesting (1973: 12) found evidence to suggest that 'An individual's use of recreation facilities is related to his "personal communities", [that is] the influence of his family, friends, workmates, and relatives.' Holman and Epperson (1984), reviewing the literature about family life cycle and leisure, suggest that the amount of time for leisure, the types of activities chosen, the frequency of participation, and the social orientation of participation (that is, which other partners are involved in the recreation activity) are variables which seem to be influenced by the developmental stage of the family. They recommend that researchers use more specific measures than simply 'stage' of the life cycle, and that different family types and activity patterns are investigated in analyses of family and leisure.

Specific interaction patterns in the relationship between husbands and wives have been hypothesized to affect leisure sociability and recreation participation. Orthner (1976) studied the extent of joint participation by spouses in recreation activities, comparing leisure behavior with the amount of communication and task-sharing in the marriage. His results indicate that 'interaction in leisure is related to interaction in marriage, but this varies over the marital career' (p. 98). Orthner and Mancini (1978) questioned whether learning specific interaction patterns during leisure as a child member of a family social group later influenced 'marital sociability' (defined as the proportion of available discretionary time spent with one's spouse during a given time period; p. 365). They concluded that 'Marital sociability may be more dependent on a constellation of factors currently operating in a marriage than in parental role modelling' (p. 369).

While these two studies are notable for their conceptual focus on interaction processes relative to leisure, they suffer from weak conceptualization of key variables (interaction, sociability, leisure), and fall victim to what may be called the 'more is better' syndrome. More task-sharing, more communication, and more activities done together are valued as 'more desirable' when, in fact, no evidence is given to justify that claim. Moreover, it is unclear whether more or better interaction leads to improved and/or more frequent leisure, or vice versa. Future research should attempt to operationalize these concepts more precisely.

One topic that has recently gained renewed attention in research about leisure is aging. Researchers interested in the importance of social relationships for personal health and happiness have begun to ask questions about how leisure facilitates the stabilization of relational ties that may influence social well-being. Specific attention has been devoted to the relationship between aging and participation in nonwork activities (McAvoy, 1979; Cohen-Mansfield, 1989; Mannell and Zuzanek, 1991), and between leisure and life satisfaction of older persons (Guinn, 1980; Ragheb and Griffeth, 1982; Kelly, 1986; Kelly *et al.*, 1987). While the current research on aging is primarily exploratory, this area of study is a potentially rich combination of the social groups and family life cycle models. Kelly and Ross (1989) have outlined a research agenda for the study of leisure in later life which includes analysis of the interaction potential of social relationships.

Summary

The basic sociological orientation towards leisure as a social context separate from work is reinforced in the types of questions that have guided research over the past quarter-century. Basic research locates leisure in the individual, and asks questions about the independent realities of time, activity, or attitude that are assumed to be experienced differently by people of different demographic, socioeconomic, and psychological characteristics. Researchers are expected to 'discover' leisure reality by studying participants whose behavior is determined by recreation contexts. These research efforts represent an empirical positivism based on a rational, mechanistic model of leisure systems.

The social groups and life cycle concepts illustrate the beginnings of a reinterpretation of reality by acknowledging the importance of others in the leisure experience. While some of the early social groups studies concentrated on describing the composition of groups at leisure settings, later studies began to consider the social processes by which such primary groups maintained solidarity. Researchers hypothesized that different kinds of social groups exhibited different organizing processes, patterns of communication, and rules of behavior, and, therefore, displayed variations in recreation behaviors. In these models, reality is seen as a subjective accomplishment – not independent of human intention, but created by people in the context of interpersonal relationships with family and friends enacted during leisure. Leisure is conceived as a social experience, not an independent object such as time, activity, or feeling.

The importance of the social groups and family life cycle concepts should not be underestimated. These models redirected the research focus in the sociology of leisure away from analyses of the characteristics of individuals, and toward analyses of the characteristics of people in relation to others in their primary groups during leisure. New interactionist perspectives about leisure were suggested, moving the research agenda from description to prediction. These models mark a philosophical turning point as well as a change in empirical approaches to studying leisure. Recreation and leisure were newly conceived as social phenomena intentionally created by people who have memberships within primary social groups.

Discussion

However promising the primary groups models of leisure appear, though, they fall short of providing a comprehensive sociology of leisure. These models have remained wedded to the analysis of the behavior of individuals in bounded, small groups. The models provide a taxonomy of potential primary groups (family, friends, mixed family and friends groups) through which people organize for leisure, but ignore other important issues, such as non-group influences on leisure, the processes by which leisure becomes institutionalized across society, and the broader social structures in which groups are embedded. A theory of leisure remains unspecified.

The primary group models are particularly problematic because few studies consider the implications of social ties beyond the group boundary. But individuals do not only live in groups, or families, or activity settings, and groups do not exist in isolation from other levels of social organization. People also live in 'social worlds' that contain a multitude of others, from strangers to intimates, and some of these others are also interconnected. Before, during, and after leisure participation, people stand in relation to one another socially. As suggested by Burch's personal communities hypothesis, people have a variety of social ties outside their leisure commitments, and these relationships probably influence the development and organization of the groupings seen at recreation places.

The primary group models, however, impose on leisure behavior a type of

'Noah's Ark' explanation. In the same way that animals are said to have walked, two by two, into the Ark, recreationists are seen to go, social group by social group, to leisure places. From a practical standpoint, it is clear that people do not simply appear onsite at recreation places, but the model leaves one wondering: How did these particular people come to be here? Where did they come from, and why did they come with these particular people and not with others? Where are they going after recreation, and how does this experience fit into their other social experiences? Despite several decades of research about leisure groups, however, researchers do not know how interaction features generate leisure groupings, how social meanings are formed and transmitted, or what group involvement means for future social commitments in broader community and society contexts.

The simple taxonomy of family, friends, or mixed groups, used in applications of the primary groups models, masks a complex arrangement of interaction patterns and relationships that may influence leisure experiences. For example, a 'group' need not always be a group. There are many different kinds of associations, including dyads, informal or casual social ties, institutionalized role relations, weak ties to associates of friends, and other kinds of ties, that probably have meaning for people in their activations of leisure choices. In addition, the tendency exhibited in most primary groups research to focus solely on small-group composition, excluding other potentially important characteristics (such as group size, communication structure, frequency of interaction, reciprocity, extended ties to others outside the group) limits social theorizing about leisure behavior.

The conception of leisure as a primary group product provides a descriptive model that bridges earlier social aggregate models and the more complex and comprehensive interactionist models that follow. Centered on the onsite, consumptive phase of recreation experiences, the value of research under the primary groups models is in stimulating thinking about the consequences of relational ties for leisure behavior. However, social group involvement should be seen as a *particular* expression of participation in wider community social relationships, rather than as the ultimate source of leisure behavior. In the next chapter, more recent interpretations and approaches to leisure are discussed, all of which draw from and extend the model of leisure as a product of primary group involvement.

3

Recent interpretive
approaches to leisure

Encounters are the guiding thread of social interaction, the succession of engagements with others ordered within the daily cycle of activity. . . . The routinization of encounters is of major significance in binding the fleeting encounter to
social reproduction and thus to the seeming 'fixity' of institutions.

(Giddens, 1984: 72)

Introduction

My grandmother was born in Rhode Island, and lived for much of her life
in a quiet neighborhood of Boston, Massachusetts. My grandfather, whom I
never knew, had left his family's farm in Ireland to look for work in the United
States when he was only 16. He and my grandmother were married in 1923;
sadly, he died in an accident at age 44 after only nine years of marriage,
leaving my grandmother with three young children. Being a single, working
parent through the 1930s and 1940s could not have been an easy life for my
grandmother. Her children – my mother, aunt, and uncle – remember a frugal
upbringing, but happy times spent in Massachusetts, Rhode Island, and
Connecticut at the homes of my grandmother's parents, sisters, and brothers.
They say that, during her 75 years, my grandmother traveled sparingly for
education and work purposes, but only once did she go on what could be
called a real 'vacation,' visiting Bermuda with her sister. Leisure, in my grandmother's day, was a family affair, and a 'local' occasion.

My mother, aunt, and uncle maintained the work ethic encouraged in their
upbringing, but grew up in a more expansive, less predictable world than my
grandmother. Theirs was the age of the automobile, the development of a
national highway system, guaranteed vacation time away from work, satellite
communications, 'nuclear' families, homes in the suburbs, more disposable

income, the emergence of television, and pleasure travel by plane. These innovations saved time and labor and created new opportunities. At the same time, a new 'consumer society' emerged, and leisure became increasingly commoditized.

The social, technological, political, and economic progress of the twentieth century restructured the relationships between people and the worlds in which they lived. My generation – my brother and sister, and my cousins – live in states 2,000 miles apart, see each other rarely, communicate by telephone and fax, and travel extensively (usually for pleasure), though generally not with one another. Our significant educational opportunities, job possibilities, and life-style choices have separated us emotionally as well as physically from one another and our families. We are independent, less 'connected' to our extended families, and unlike the lives of my grandmother and parents, it is a rare and special event when our extended families gather. For my generation, leisure seems to be centered in each individual's social and economic circumstances, not within the extended family, as it was in my grandmother's time.

On occasion, though, various life pathways and social ties intersect. In 1987 my mother and aunt traveled to County Donegal, Ireland, to visit their father's homesite. During their trip, they were guests at the home of one of my friends, a childhood schoolmate whom I have known for over 20 years. While she and I had remained in irregular contact over the years through letters and phone calls, my parents had never been close to her or to her family. Now they exchange letters and personal visits directly, and I am no longer the intermediary in their relationships. At another time and place during their trip to Ireland, my parents met some of their 'long-lost' cousins, and as a result, my mother and aunt have ties to new friends in both Ireland and the United States. In the same way that economic, social, and technological advances once created new opportunities for leisure, the resiliency of family ties, combined with the possibilities of friendship ties, continue to create new chances for our leisure today.

In itself, this story is important only as the maternal history of my own family. In a broader sense, though, it illustrates the role of leisure across several generations, and highlights the importance of social ties of history, kinship, and friendship for individual and social behavior. Disregarding for the moment that personal expectations and societal progress have changed the nature of leisure across the years, the one remaining constant is that relationships between people still play a role in defining and structuring the activities of free time. The study of leisure and society is the study of people in their search for a meaningful life, expressed and facilitated through their relationships with one another, with their society, and with the institutions that surround and contain their searching.

New Sociologies of Leisure

In the previous chapter, the formalization of sociological concepts and methods in leisure research, and early efforts to study the individual and social group characteristics of leisure behavior, were discussed. This chapter documents more recent critiques of the theoretical and methodological positions adopted in the earlier traditional approaches. Developing primarily over the past decade, these critiques stem from a growing realization of the need for more serious evaluation of the social interactions and social contexts of leisure expressions. Described as 'interpretive sociologies' of leisure because of their collective focus on personal and social constructions of leisure behavior, these new approaches are impacting the discipline by recasting issues about the people, places, and social meanings of leisure.

The introduction of the social groups, family life cycle, and social circles concepts in leisure research represented shifts away from purely individual analyses of leisure behavior and related psychological dispositions. In application, however, the social group models of leisure behavior were often overly simplistic. People do not only belong to primary groups in society: their interactions with others are varied and complex. Moreover, the use of primary group variables does not guarantee theoretical sophistication about the processes of interaction that underlay leisure behavior.

The sense that descriptive and quantitative research traditions failed to describe adequately the complexity of leisure behavior stimulated new theoretical and methodological developments. During the past decade, the ongoing debate in science about the relative merits and promise of 'qualitative' and 'quantitative' approaches has been re-enacted in leisure research. Early research traditions, centered on quantitative traditions, were criticized for neglecting issues of meaning and context in analysis of the experience of leisure. As Smith (1979: 4) argues, 'human behavior "appears" to entail elements such as intentions, meanings, values and beliefs which are not "real" in [an] object frame of reference.' Table 3.1 outlines the basic tenets of each approach (after Schwartz and Jacobs, 1979), even though it may be an artificial distinction to separate the two traditions so completely. As Giddens (1984: 333–4) points out, 'All so-called "quantitative" data, when scrutinized, turn out to be composites of "qualitative" . . . interpretations produced by situated researchers . . . qualitative and quantitative methods should be seen as complementary rather than antagonistic aspects of social research.'

The emerging set of critical and exploratory analyses of leisure are connected by the view that leisure is found not only in 'recreation events' but in the context of people's daily lives. Collectively, these new approaches incorporate a wide range of social theories and philosophical perspectives, demonstrate increased complexity in conceptualization, and begin to incorporate qualitative methods into research designs. The intent of these new approaches is to provide a more detailed understanding of the micro-level

Table 3.1 Comparisons: qualitative vs. quantitative research

Quantitative methods	Qualitative methods
1. Positivistic science	1. Interpretive science
2. Focus on 'social facts'	2. Focus on the 'actor's point of view'
3. Social reality is 'objective'; social facts are external to individuals	3. Social reality is 'subjective' and experiential; meaning is socially constructed
4. Goal: methodological and statistical rigor; empirical analysis	4. Goal: understand meanings and experiences of actors in their worlds
5. Approach: identify and measure empirical trends in the real world	5. Approach: researcher places self in the lived worlds of subjects
6. Methods: standardized techniques, survey research, questionnaires	6. Methods: nonstandardized techniques, field studies, participant observation, interviews, ethnographic case studies

interactions among social actors, focusing specifically on how people create and replicate social order and meanings during leisure experiences.

The dual problems of context and intention are particularly difficult to analyze under traditional social groups models of leisure behavior. Actions that can be called leisure take place in a social world, and are constrained and facilitated by social circumstances often beyond the control of single individuals. There is a need for research that acknowledges the influence of social context on behavior and that analyzes human intentions which produce leisure. The preeminent philosophy of the new interpretive sociologies is that leisure is 'created' by people through social interaction. Leisure is not simply an 'object' that has certain properties (duration, activity engagement, emotion) which are defined by a researcher prior to investigation.

The new interpretive sociologies include existentialism, symbolic interactionism, phenomenology, ethnomethodology, exchange theory, humanism, feminism, and preliminary work about structural influences on leisure. Research work under these approaches is critical, exploratory, and evaluative. A sampling of literature using these approaches is presented below; a further exposition of some of these ideas can be found in a special issue of the *Journal of Leisure Research* (1990, Vol. 22, No. 4). While leisure scholars tend to refer to these new approaches as 'interpretive' researches, it should be noted that other authors employ the term 'interpretative' sociologies (see, for example, Giddens, 1976, 1984). In practice, both terms refer to 'schools of thought . . . that have certain shared concerns with "meaningful action" ' (Giddens, 1976: 8), and are often used interchangeably.

Alternative theories and methods

Many of the new interpretive approaches in leisure research incorporate symbolic interaction theories and ethnographic methods. Symbolic interactionism is a perspective linked with several prominent social theorists in Europe and America, most notably Georg Simmel, George Herbert Mead, and Mead's student Herbert Blumer (Blumer, 1969; Turner, 1982; Collins, 1985). This perspective assumes that, through their use of symbolic communication in social interaction, humans continually create meanings about their world and about their actions in the world. Interaction is mediated by role-taking, in which individuals anticipate the responses of others, and more fully define and develop their own self-concepts. Social behavior becomes a process of defining situations by interpreting symbols and adopting appropriate behavior strategies (Blumer, 1969).

The assumptions of symbolic interactionism call for methods of induction that allow researchers to explore fluid processes of social involvement, including self-concept development, role-taking behavior, and the interactions of small sets of people engaged in personal relationships. The methods include intensive case studies or exploratory research using techniques of participant observation, depth interviewing, analytic induction, or descriptive ethnographies (Schwartz and Jacobs, 1979; Lincoln and Guba, 1985). These more 'qualitative' approaches differ dramatically from the survey research tradition in leisure and recreation research, a tradition that persisted even in many of the earlier studies about the leisure involvements of primary groups of families and friends.

In leisure research, symbolic interactionism has received widespread use from researchers interested in describing the small-group contexts, interactive nature, and role performances of leisure and tourist behaviors. Some of these concerns were previously articulated by researchers studying small groups and family contexts of leisure who raised questions about the identities people create and the roles they assume in the performance of leisure. A more formal discussion of leisure applications of symbolic interactionism was outlined by Kelly (1983), whose book *Leisure Identities and Interactions* presented a comprehensive discussion of leisure styles and contexts through life.

Other authors have also discussed applications of symbolic interactionism in leisure research. Colton (1987) reviewed literature using symbolic interactionist approaches in leisure, recreation, and tourism. Samdahl (1988) discussed the requirements of a symbolic interactionist theory of leisure, and tested propositions relating social roles and personal expression to the experience of leisure. She noted that 'leisure can be viewed as a distinctive pattern of perceiving and relating to ongoing interaction . . . a particular definition of the situation' (*ibid.*: 29). The processes of self-concept development and self-awareness through leisure involvement were also discussed by Samdahl and Kleiber (1989). In the tourism literature, MacCannell's (1976) analyses of authenticity issues in front- and back-stage tourism settings, modeled on Goffman's work, represent a most complete statement of interactionist theorizing.

Phenomenological theorizing has also recently received attention from leisure researchers. The German philosopher Husserl provided the initial statement of 'transcendental consciousness' that was later developed more fully as a sociological perspective by Alfred Schutz (Wagner, 1970; Stewart and Mickunas, 1974; Luckmann, 1978). Phenomenology takes interactionist theorizing to another level by proposing that 'the subjective world of actors is a reality in itself' (Turner, 1982: 389). Researchers using phenomenological approaches study social relationships that make up the common, everyday worlds of people in an effort to understand the ways by which people create social reality and the social actions that affirm reality conceptions (Wagner, 1970; Filstead, 1976). In leisure research, Harper (1981, 1986) proposed utilizing a method of 'descriptive phenomenology' to understand leisure as individual experience. While he does not explicitly describe procedures for conducting such an analysis, he does suggest that phenomenology can provide the basis for deriving testable hypotheses about the 'basic structure of lived experience' (1981: 120). His sentiments are echoed by Dawson (1984), who also calls for the application of phenomenological approaches in analyzing leisure and recreation activities.

Feminist critiques, and analyses of women's leisure more generally, have also gained a new prominence in the literature (Shaw, 1985b; Allison and Duncan, 1987; Henderson, 1990, 1991a). Supported by feminist theories, and often qualitative in nature, much of this research shows that women have life experiences that cannot easily be separated into discrete categories called 'work' and 'leisure.' For example, Henderson and Rannells (1988: 41), in a sample of farm women, discovered that 'women found meaning and leisure through an integration of work, family, and community experiences.'

The new feminist research is especially interesting in perspective, and draws attention to the leisure of a significant subset of the population. However, feminist research in leisure currently can be seen as primarily a critical viewpoint, rather than a full theory of gender differences. Since previous studies in leisure research used samples containing both men and women, and since much of the qualitative research about women's leisure uses very small samples, it is unclear whether the differences in leisure behaviors and meanings are due to methodological approach or represent real contrasts. However intuitively correct the findings might seem to women, there remains a need for comparative research, using both qualitative as well as quantitative research, to analyze gender differences in leisure.

One final approach that deserves mention is exchange theory. Based on notions of utility, and assuming that people will attempt to maximize rewards through negotiation in social relationships (Turner, 1982), exchange theory has been proposed as a way to explain people's decisions to cease participation in leisure activities (Searle, 1991), and as a means of understanding host-guest relationships in tourist communities. At this time, exchange theory has received only limited attention from leisure researchers, but remains an interesting avenue for future research.

Many of the new interpretive sociologies of leisure, deriving from a world view in which social actors are seen as creating the realities they live, require qualitative methods. Research questions differ from traditional positivistic approaches, and methods of data collection and analysis are correspondingly varied. Several of the studies noted above combine qualitative with quantitative approaches or are entirely qualitative. Specific applications of qualitative research in leisure are addressed by Howe (1988) and Henderson (1991b).

Expanded levels of analysis

Not only are theoretical perspectives under revision in the sociology of leisure, but the social contexts of leisure experience are also being debated more vigorously. Researchers are no longer content to assume that primary social groups comprising family and friends are the only, or the most important, influence on an individual's leisure behavior. Researchers currently look to other levels of social order, such as common occasions, informal associations, collectives, and social worlds, to document and analyze the role and meaning of leisure experiences in people's lives.

The idea of 'common leisure occasions' places leisure experiences in the 'informal, unstructured . . . situations which emerge throughout daily life' (Samdahl, 1992: 19). In contrast to specific recreation events, leisure is seen as an emergent experience in an individual's daily routines. Samdahl (*ibid.*: 30) proposed that the informal social interaction possibilities of common leisure occasions 'allows the presentation and validation of one's true self,' contributing to a more complete social definition of leisure behavior.

In a more formal vein, Hoggett and Bishop (1985) and Pine (1984) suggest a need to look at the voluntary sector of leisure involvement – clubs, groups, and informal associations – through which individuals build meaningful communal affiliations during leisure. Alternatively, Heywood (1988: 119) uses Parsons's theory of voluntaristic action to describe the characteristics of 'leisure collectives' which are 'made up of combinations of known and unknown others, who join together to pursue a recreation activity for one time, then disband never to exist again.' The broader social contexts described in these approaches confirm that leisure experience is not based only in primary group membership.

One of the most innovative applications of interpretive theorizing in leisure research has been the recent attention to the 'social worlds' of participants (Ditton *et al.*, 1992). The concept of social worlds has been defined in social psychology as 'an internally recognizable constellation of actors, organizations, events and practices that have coalesced into a perceived sphere of interest and involvement' (Unruh, 1979: 115). In research about social worlds, symbolic interaction theories are generally applied in an effort to uncover how members of social worlds establish roles and meanings through communication and shared participation. DeVall (1976) provided one of the first analyses of the social worlds of leisure, analyzing both surfers and mountain climbers. Walter (1984) also examined the social worlds of climbers, extending his analysis to consider the vicarious experience of mountain climbing by nonmountaineer observers. A more urban view of social worlds was presented in Smith's (1985) participant observation of a working-class pub.

More recently, Glancy (1988, 1990) studied the social world of auctions to determine how roles developed among participants, and how people became 'players' in the activities of the auction setting. Scott and Godbey (1992) analyzed the play world of adult bridge groups, describing the differences between serious and social bridge clubs and players. They comment that the social worlds concept provides two perspectives for studying leisure: researchers can analyze either the shared experiences of 'local' social groups, or can broaden their analyses to consider 'the play group . . . against a backdrop of practices and events in the broader social world and in intersecting social worlds in which group members participate' (p. 64).

The idea that people have multiple social ties across varied social world commitments is exactly the premise of research about communities of affiliation and social networks. Levy (1989) and Stokowski and Lee (1991) discuss these issues in detail, and their work, along with other social network analyses in leisure, is presented and evaluated in Chapter 6.

While analyses about levels of social organization beyond primary groups shows promise for increasing understanding of leisure behavior, many of the studies remain focused on within-group (club, team, organization) activity and relationships. If broader social structural concerns are mentioned, it is only in passing, with speculative comments about between-groups linkages. For example, Scott and Godbey (1992: 63) acknowledge that 'play groups should be conceived and analyzed as local social worlds that are linked to broader, more conclusive social world systems,' but they do not specify any theory or method for linking local groups across society. Since the issue of levels of analysis is important in the study of networks, it will be addressed further in later chapters.

Reframing issues

The new interpretive sociologies of leisure are having an impact on traditional understandings of leisure phenomena. New questions are raised about the social enactment of leisure and the consequences of personal relationships for leisure behavior. In addition to describing the multiple social contexts of leisure, researchers have also become interested in the nature of meanings created through leisure, and the role of leisure in contributing to a meaningful life. Some of these questions were also raised in earlier work about social groups and family involvement in leisure. For example, Lee (1972) suggested that meanings attributed to leisure are created by social groups who use outdoor recreation areas for different purposes. These leisure meanings subsequently become institutionalized across recreation subcultures.

More recently, Howe (1985) outlined a qualitative paradigm for analyzing individual leisure meanings in coordination with their social, behavioral outcomes. Shaw (1985a) used a symbolic interactionist approach to study the meaning of leisure in people's everyday lives, analyzing meaning as an individual 'definition' of a situation. Hemingway (1990) described how meanings and actions arise from the intersubjective social practices of individuals. Williams *et al.* (1992) attempted to relate patterns of 'place attachment' to the performance of recreation behaviors at wilderness settings. They define meanings as 'emotional and symbolic values of natural resources' (p. 29), and use scaled response items in surveys to correlate meanings with behaviors. Their work is a preliminary attempt to quantify the phenomenological basis of individual place attachments in natural resource areas.

As interpretive perspectives become more common in the sociology of leisure, research will likely center on three topics: (1) processes of creation and elaboration of personal identity through leisure; (2) the mechanisms by which group involvement enables or constrains appropriate roles and social behaviors; and (3) the processes by which social meanings are produced and confirmed through interaction. Several of these topics have been addressed in preliminary ways and are receiving new interest from researchers. For example, identity affirmation and self-concept development were issues addressed by primary groups researchers, and more recently by Haggard and Williams (1992) and Shamir (1992). In addition, a large body of research about encounter norms thought to derive from group involvement at outdoor recreation settings has accumulated (for example, see Whittaker and Shelby, 1988; Roggenbuck *et al.*, 1991; Noe, 1992).

Discussion

Traditional approaches in the sociology of leisure view leisure as nonrandom social behavior that has inherent meaning for participants and for society. Early research in the sociology of leisure confirmed that the social phenomenon called leisure comprised recreation activities which occurred in 'free time' (i.e., nonwork time). Leisure experiences were also assumed to result in pleasurable sentiments and feelings for participants. And researchers proposed that leisure had a structure different from other social involvements: people were usually involved in leisure as members of social groups rather than as single individuals.

Recent interpretive sociologies of leisure reinforce and expand these traditional foci. Primary group influences on individual leisure behavior are still of interest to researchers, but new theoretical and methodological perspectives raise different issues and research questions. Interpretive perspectives begin with the assumption that leisure is not only produced through involvement in specific recreation events but also emerges from the circumstances of daily life. Further, leisure is not an isolated context of life, producing various psychological states for individuals, but derives from complex social relationships and interactions. As Kelly (1982: 111) comments, 'If leisure is social interaction, relationships, and the expression of community, then we need to know about stability and change in social contexts, about groups, normative expectations, self-presentations, the regularities of institutions, and the meanings of life together.'

While interpretive perspectives have advanced social theorizing about leisure behavior, they still can be considered only partial attempts at a comprehensive structural sociology of leisure. Regardless of the social context analyzed, researchers still tend to reduce findings to the level of the individual and his or her sociopsychological characteristics. The focus on micro-level interactions is akin to looking at isolated pieces of a puzzle rather than at the puzzle in entirety. The analytic process ignores broader questions about the role of leisure across society, the location of individuals in extended social structures, and the influence of structure on behavior.

These criticisms are echoed by Kelly (1992), one of the foremost leisure sociologists in the United States, in a recent provocative critique of the sociology of leisure. He notes that leisure is complex, social, and contextual, and that 'concentration on individual experience places leisure in a cocoon of private feelings and meanings' (p. 252). Leisure, he says, 'is action *in* structure. . . . [Leisure is] produced by action in the real world of roles and responsibilities as well as of division by race, class, age, and gender' (p. 249). Kelly's comments highlight some of the personal and social considerations known to affect leisure experiences, framing these explicitly in structural terms.

While both social positions and involvement in social relationships can be assumed to influence leisure choices, analyses of structural features have been largely ignored by leisure researchers. Absent from our understanding of leisure as a socially significant phenomenon is knowledge of how the social relationships surrounding individuals, from close to distant ties, in formal or informal organization, form broad networks of others who may potentially influence leisure.

A comprehensive sociology of leisure demands explanations of the social contexts and social meanings of leisure, and the institutionalization of leisure across society. A three-part research imperative is required. First, researchers need to study leisure not only as an object but also as a context of social experience within which social processes develop. These contexts occur at various levels of social organization, not simply within the setting of bounded, small social groups. While family and friends play an important role in leisure, these significant others are not the only ones who may influence an individual's leisure choices. Interactionist theories, in conjunction with broader structural theories about social order, are required.

Second, it is important to account for 'time' as an element in the social context of leisure, in that behaviors and meanings of leisure have both a past and a future coherence rather than simply an onsite performance. Third, there is a need to shift attention away from the characteristics of individuals or groups as the unit of analysis, and focus on characteristics of social relationships between people. This effort is consistent with interpretive perspectives which claim that it is within the context of interpersonal relationships that leisure is made socially real.

People have social histories. They do not simply appear during free time in leisure settings to take part in activities which give them good feelings. Further, their leisure experiences are enacted from within multiple social contexts of life. People come from some place first, and are returning somewhere after recreation involvement. Along the way they are meeting, traveling with, visiting, conversing with, watching, and listening to other people. Traditional approaches in the sociological study of leisure fail to consider that people stand in relation to one another socially, before, during, and after leisure experiences.

It is in this respect that social relationships provide the basic structure, order, and coherence to make leisure and recreation real and meaningful. In turn, relationships are replicated, patterned, and institutionalized across society, forming systems of interaction and meaning. A comprehensive sociology of leisure must include analyses of the structured interpersonal and community relationships that provide the foundation and coherence for individual and social leisure behaviors.

In this regard, a sociology of leisure should not be only a study of primary groups but must also include the study of social positions and relationships that stem from a variety of communal contexts. Many arrangements of formal and informal social organization have potential importance for leisure. In addition to the organizing contexts identified earlier (primary groups, social circles, social worlds, and others), leisure behaviors may emerge from relationships between persons in dyads, extended ties with small and large social groups and cliques, stronger and weaker ties with significant others, formal organizational affiliation, and other general ties of sociability.

Sociological thinking about leisure must be concerned with how the extended range of social positions and relationships surrounding an individual might encourage or prohibit recreation opportunities. As used here, the term 'extended relationships' refers to persistent patterns of relational linkages among people that comprise 'social networks' on the macro level of society. The arrangement and meaning of a person's social relationships, both within and outside of leisure, and the location of those patterns across broader systems of interaction, should be the focus of research attention in the sociology of leisure.

4

Elements of a structural sociology of leisure

The technician and the astrologer, no less than the rest of us, are pattern intoxi-
cated: Reading the charts or the stars, they see the subtle seams by which things
are constructed. A pattern is peculiar in that knowing part of the pattern one
is likely to guess correctly at the rest. In this sense, the concept of a pattern is
tied to the concept of a regularity, and beyond that to the concept of unalter-
ability. The rising and the setting sun, the turbid ebb and flow of human relationships, the course of disease, all form measured and distinctive patterns; it is their
inevitability that gives us that heartfelt hiccupping pause when she says with a
catch in her throat that Ralph We Have to Talk.

(Berlinski, 1986: 76)

Introduction

The term 'social structure' is a central concept in sociological reasoning
(Macksey and Donato, 1972; Turner, 1982; Wellman and Berkowitz, 1988b).
Given its importance, one would expect that the concept of structure would
be well defined and well understood, but this is not always the case. In the
following pages, sociological approaches to the specification of the concept
of social structure are considered, and elements of a structural sociology of
leisure are discussed.

Social Structure

Turner (1982: 444) refers to social structure as '*the* subject matter of sociology'
but acknowledges that 'the notion of structure remains somewhat vague.' The
concept of social structure is particularly problematic for researchers because,
while the term has been applied in a variety of ways (Blau, 1975), it is often
incompletely defined or lacking in theoretical consistency. Further, scholars

are apt to revise their ideas over time, and thus no single definition does justice to the depth of reasoning inherent in a particular perspective. Some general approaches to the idea of social structure, representing diverse perspectives and orientations in social theory, can be identified, however, and have been outlined in Table 4.1. This table is not meant to be all-inclusive; the selection of definitions is intended only to illuminate a range of theoretical approaches.

Structural theorists have used the term structure in reference to both concrete social objects (for example, groups or organizations have been described as 'structures'), to more abstract social processes that cannot be seen directly (such as the patterning of relationships across social networks), or sometimes even to social aggregates (individuals grouped on the basis of some social characteristic, such as education level). Giddens (1976: 120-1) argues, however, that 'A structure is not a "group", "collectivity", or "organization": these *have* structures. Groups and collectivities can and should be studied as systems of interactions.'

A basic definition in a sociology text defines social structure as 'the relatively predictable and continuing patterns of human relationships and interactions . . . among individuals and groups that enables them to function as a society' (Coser *et al.*, 1987: 632). The characteristics and processes of social structure may be studied under a variety of theories in sociology. For example, Blau (1982) describes at least four types of structural perspectives: Marx's theory of production relations, class and society; Parsons's structural functionalism based on social system integration; Lévi-Strauss's 'deep structure' of language and human cognition; and the new network structuralism, which is concerned with the distribution and patterns of social positions and relationships across society. Taken together, these perspectives imply that there is no single structure to social behavior, and that social structures are relative and can be viewed from a variety of organizational levels.

The variable nature of social structure results both from the complexity of social environments and from people's abilities both to engage in and to give meaning to their social involvements. Tiryakian (1970: 115) points out that structures are social creations, saying, 'Social structures [are] normative phenomena of intersubjective consciousness which frame social actions in social space.' Interactions among people form the basis for the creation of social meanings about relations between objects, and these meanings support future social action.

The importance of studying social structure is given in the assumption that 'structures' might not only contain human behaviors but may also influence human behavior. Marsden and Lin (1982: 9) comment that 'The premise that behaviors or actions are interpretable only in relation to the positions of actors in social structure underlies much social scientific inquiry.' Actors, of course, may be people at any level of social organization, from individuals in dyadic relationships to corporate actors, such as bureaucratic organizations or

Table 4.1 What is social structure?

Author	Definition
Blau, re Marx (1982: 273)	'The "late Marx" [is] a structural theory, which explains other aspects of society – religion, politics, family, folkways, mores – in terms of its infrastructure, which entails notably productive forces, people's relations of production, and the resulting class structure.'
Blau, re Parsons (1982: 274)	'Structure [in Parsons's structural functionalism] pertains to the interrelated institutional subsystems of value and normative orientation. . . . [According to Parsons] social structure refers to "the conditions involved in the interaction of actual human individuals who constitute concrete collectivities with determinate memberships".'
Lévi-Strauss (cited in Macksey and Donato, 1972: 232)	'If the structure can be seen, it will not be at the . . . empirical level, but at a deeper one . . . that of unconscious categories.'
Radcliffe-Brown (in Leinhardt, 1977: 224)	'In the study of social structure, the concrete reality with which we are concerned is the set of actually existing relations, at a given moment of time which link together certain human beings.'
Blumer (1969: 6–7)	'Social structure in any of its aspects, as represented by such terms as social position, status, role, authority, and prestige, refers to relationships derived from how people act toward one another. . . . A cardinal principle of symbolic interactionism is that any empirically oriented scheme of human society . . . must respect the fact that in the first and last instances human society consists of people engaging in action.'
Homans (in Blau, 1975: 63–4)	'Structures are the relatively permanent features of societies and groups whose characteristics and interrelations we intend to describe, analyze, and explain. Structures are the subject-matter of sociologists of many different methodological and theoretical persuasions . . .'
Giddens (1976: 127)	'By the term "structure" I do not refer, as is conventional in functionalism, to the descriptive analysis of the relations of interaction which "compose" organizations or collectivities, but to systems of generative rules and resources . . . structures only exist as the reproduced conduct of situated actors with definite intentions and interests.'
Wellman and Berkowitz (1988a: 3)	'Structural analysts . . . [study] "social structures" directly and concretely [by analyzing] the ordered arrangements of relations that are contingent upon exchange among members of social systems.'

nations. Social structures do not have to be visible to the naked eye in order to have implications for individual or collective behavior.

While some versions of structural theorizing are deterministic (i.e., proposing that individual behavior is caused by structural forces), recent trends in structural analysis represent efforts to evaluate the reciprocal influences of social structure on individual behavior, and of behavior on social structure. These issues move the concept of social structure into the debate about micro–macro linkages in social science.

Micro–macro linkages

The division between micro and macro levels of social organization is fundamentally a question about the integration of, and relations between, individuals and society. While, individually, people 'meet' reality on micro, personal levels, does it follow that 'Macro structure consists of nothing more than large numbers of microencounters, repeated . . . over time and space' (Collins, 1987: 195)? Most theorists would agree that the relation between action and structure is more than simply a matter of aggregating events, numbers, or characteristics of people. However, the manner in which the small-scale social processes of micro-level interactions translate into, or coalesce into, macro-level phenomena remains unresolved (Alexander *et al.*, 1987).

As a discipline, sociology forces the question of how to understand the activities of individuals in light of the behavior of collectivities, and vice versa. Alexander and Giesen (1987: 13) note that 'The question of order for sociology concerns the ultimate source of social patterns . . . [which] may be conceived individualistically [or] as emanating from some (collective) source outside any particular individual.' They point out that sociology, by its focus on empirical (not only philosophical) analyses, has a range of theoretical options for dealing with problems of order and scale. For example, individuals might be seen to create order purposefully, or they might 'give in' to social forces which control them. Between these two extremes, several other options exist for people to interpret, or to reproduce, society depending on their level of control. The current intellectual debate in sociology, though, centers not on the primacy of any one of these options over the others but on the synthesis of alternatives (Munch and Smelser, 1987).

In its most basic form, the micro–macro debate is about the organization of social actors and social action. Micro-level relationships between people form the basis for macrostructural organization among social actors and their social creations, which include the patterning and distribution of resources, myths, meanings, authority, or norms of public behavior. The underlying theme of the micro–macro debate is that reciprocal influence exists between individual action and structural order. Social order arises and is reproduced, intentionally or unintentionally, from micro-level encounters between people; reciprocally, the behavior of individuals is influenced by their positions in social structure. Beyond simply analyzing phenomena at each level, one of the tasks of sociological research is to describe more completely the intersections between micro (relational) and macro (structural) levels of social organization.

The Social Structures of Leisure

The discussion of relational and structural processes in society has relevance for leisure phenomena. Questions of social structure (beyond, that is, social class characteristics of recreationists, or structures of specific leisure groups) are generally ignored in leisure research. The research agenda of leisure has developed at the micro level of analysis with little attention to macro-level structures of institutionalized social relationships in leisure. Traditional and interactionist research concludes that leisure is relational, but there is little subsequent effort to understand the reproduction of leisure relationships throughout society.

How does social structure enter into leisure behavior and meaning? First, structural research seeks to explain the patterning of interactions across systems in their entirety. This is an effort at description: how are relationships ordered across contexts, and how are particular kinds of relationships juxtaposed against others? Second, structural research attempts to understand how actors vary and manipulate their relationships in order to create structures that optimize their goals. Social interactions are not only happenstance but are also the direct result of actors' intentions. Third, structural research examines the relational patterns resulting from intentional and unintentional action in an effort to predict how the arrangement of elements within and across social systems influences the behaviors of contributing social actors.

This research process should not be interpreted as a search for an ultimate, single 'structure of leisure' in society, but as the search for understanding the reciprocal effects of social structures on behavior, and of personal behavior on structures. To adopt a phenomenological view, relational interactions are always subject to re-creation in new social settings, and social structures are likewise always being modified. Adopting a structural position, which assumes that there are regularities in the way social actions and interactions are performed, suggests that general patterns of behavior and meaning can be uncovered in research.

An understanding of social structure begins with two general kinds of theories: those that explore relational elements that support social action, and those that seek to explain structural influences on social action. In the following sections of this chapter, basic relational elements of a structural sociology of leisure will be presented, and issues related to structural research in leisure will be discussed. In the next chapter, a specific method for analyzing social structure, social network analysis, is introduced. Applications of this method to leisure behavior are discussed in later chapters.

Social relationships

The concept of 'relationship' figures prominently in sociological and anthropological research (McCall *et al.*, 1970). Relationships are connections or linkages between two or more social 'actors' who may be individuals, groups, or larger collectivities such as industries or nations (McCall and Simmons, 1978). In daily life, relationships provide meaning, stability, and order for human social interactions (Berger and Kellner, 1964). Over time, relationships that are significant to people tend to be reproduced, and their occurrence and outcomes can thus be predicted.

In both popular and academic circles, the term 'relation' (for example, 'role relation') is often used interchangeably with the term 'relationship'. Mundackal (1977), however, suggests that relations are more objective, while the idea of a relationship implies a personal or subjective quality of interaction. In analyzing Martin Buber's philosophy, he explains that

> If questions are asked about a person's relation with other men, information is usually required as to whether he is friendly, cruel or kind to them, and whether they like or dislike him, trust or distrust him, and so on. Attention is thus being drawn to his attitudes towards them and their reactions to him. . . . ['Relation-ship'] suggests something more structured that grows up between or is entered into by two men and in which there is some element of reciprocity and openness, and which arises from the initiative of the individuals concerned, not from some impersonal order arising from role, convention, or morality. (p. 75)

The distinction between the two terms is generally clear in application. For example, people usually stand in relation to their bus driver or grocery clerk but maintain relationships with their spouse and friends. Qualities of relations are understood objectively, by observing and reacting to the positions of others in impersonal ways. On the other hand, relationships have phenome-nological qualities. People willingly and subjectively participate in a mutual attempt to 'take the part of' the other, to narrow the social and psychological 'distance' between themselves, and to create cooperatively shared realities.

The importance of relationships in sociology is that interpersonal ties come to have meaning for participants in their construction of lived realities (Buber, 1965; Theunissen, 1986). Berger and Kellner (1964: 1) note that relationships are

> social arrangements that create for the individual the sort of order in which he can experience his life as making sense. . . . In a broad sense, *all* the other cohabitants of this world serve a validating function . . . however, some valida-tions are more significant than others.

Coleman (1975: 82), citing the work of Abel, points out that sociologists traditionally distinguish between two kinds of relationships: interest relation-ships (those 'in which a relation is a means to an end for a member of it'), and sentiment relationships ('in which the relation is an end in itself'). These two kinds of relationships reflect general orientations of each actor toward the other. In addition to these basic orientations, the literature about social rela-tionships suggests that single ties between people can contain many types of relational contents (Wellman, 1979; Milardo, 1988a), and common sense bears this out. Siblings might also be best friends, work associates might be fun to socialize with, and friends might provide emotional and tangible support in addition to socializing opportunities. Since people may be involved in a multitude of relationships at any given time, it is important that researchers be able to distinguish among different types of relationships, and also be able to define the range of relational contacts that are presupposed in each.

The study of relational contents is driven by theories about the functions and meanings of different types of relationships for people. Exchange relationships, for example, presuppose theories of interpersonal and collective behavior that focus on the value of objects across transactions. Market relations are a type of exchange, for example, between producers and consumers. Sentiment relationships presuppose theories of affect, liking, and friendship, and are generally linked with noninstrumental behaviors conducted within the realm of free choice. Power relationships presuppose theories of control and coordination of behavior based on status differentials between social actors who may be either individuals or corporate actors. For all types of relationships, important questions on the micro level center around the issues of meaning (what is the immediate meaning of a relationship to participants at a given time?) and activation (under what circumstances are different relationships activated for different purposes?).

Relationships of leisure
The first goal in developing a structural sociology of leisure is describing the qualities of relationships activated for leisure purposes. There is likely no such thing as a single 'leisure relationship.' Rather, people are involved in many relationships at once, and relationships from across life contexts are probably differentially activated for leisure purposes.

Traditional and interactionist theorizing in leisure research has uncovered several consistencies about leisure relationships. First, leisure relationships are described as being affective and pleasurable in nature. Leisure is assumed to have positive social connotations where 'liking' (or at least not 'disliking') the others involved is the norm. The literature suggests that people exercise freedom of choice in leisure, and it is unlikely that individuals would repeatedly or freely seek leisure opportunities with others they dislike.

Second, the research literature suggests that affective relationships of leisure tend to be organized informally and weakly institutionalized in social life. Previous research indicates that these relationships are played out in relatively small interpersonal, group, or cluster configurations of daily life. Unlike other contexts of human life, such as work or school, leisure behavior does not at first glance seem to be coordinated by formal institutions and hierarchies that persist despite member turnover. The research literature locates leisure behavior and the experiences of leisure in the micro-structures of interpersonal relationships, where meanings are constructed rather than imposed by outside forces.

Third, leisure may be hypothesized to involve specifically noninstrumental social relationships. Kelly (1982: 115) points out that 'Leisure is distinguished from work, not by being satisfying or enjoyable, but by its lack of a product of economic or social value.' That is, social relationships in the context of leisure are entered into for their own sake, rather than for instrumental purposes. Leisure relationships are informal and voluntary. This quality is assumed to differentiate between social relationships of leisure and other kinds of relationships, such as exchange relationships. The literature about leisure is unclear, however, regarding whether or to what extent sentiment and exchange relationships might overlap.

Realistically, there are probably many instances where instrumental and exchange relationships overlap with relationships of sentiment during leisure. For example, a corporate executive who invites a client or business colleague to play golf is clearly not acting solely on the basis of sentiment. If he or she were, then only clients or colleagues to whom the executive had strong attachments would be invited to play. In fact, though, others without such attachments are sometimes invited, and the potential for furthering business contacts or entering into sales arrangements figures prominently in the executive's decision to choose specific others as golf partners. According to prevailing theories of leisure, it is questionable whether these golf relations should be considered 'leisure' relationships, even though they do result in recreation activities.

However, one could make the argument that all social relationships, including those of sentiment and affection, contain some elements of purposefulness or instrumentality. It is necessary in this case to make a distinction between the general character of a relationship and how that relationship is enacted from moment to moment. The 'general character' of a relationship may be defined as the 'type' of relation, or the positions or roles of the participants, as evident to others. That is, relationships occur between parents and children, between friends, and between bosses and employees, and these are called, respectively, kinship, friendship, and superior–subordinate relations. On the other hand, how relationships are enacted from moment to moment is at least partially the result of qualities of mutuality that arise between specific people in whatever kinds of relative positions they maintain.

For example, friendship is not, on a day-to-day basis, only a matter of mutual sentiment. Friends rely on one another for information, advice, emotional support, comfort, and perhaps special services, such as house-sitting or small errands. The mutuality of friendships does not diminish the instrumentality of friendly relations; rather, it adds another layer of depth to such relationships. On the other hand, predominantly instrumental relations (such as that of the corporate executive and client) may also contain elements of voluntary engagement that are at least partly outside the bounds of instrumentality inherent in the relation.

The conclusion of this line of reasoning is that, contrary to current thinking about leisure, relationships should not be defined as *either* instrumental *or* noninstrumental. Rather, it could be hypothesized that a continuum exists between the two extremes, and that leisure behaviors may arise when predominantly noninstrumental aspects of *any* kinds of relationships are enacted. This hypothesis allows that leisure relationships might occur in work environments and in other situations where instrumental relations are generally the norm. Thus it is not inconsistent to conceive of leisure opportunities between corporate executives and clients or business partners who otherwise have formal business relations.

Finally, in addition to the individual qualities and meanings of specific social relationships activated for leisure purposes, relationships are also significant in the aggregate. People live in complex social worlds, and maintain simultaneous relationships with family, friends, neighbors, colleagues, and others in their personal and home communities. Relationships are both accumulated and lost over time, and the entire set of relational ties 'belonging' to an individual at any given time probably influences at least some opportunities for leisure behavior. While only a small proportion of a person's social ties are likely to be enacted for leisure choices, it is reasonable to ask how and why some relationships, and not others, develop for leisure purposes and, correspondingly, how social ties enacted in leisure settings influence future personal and community relationships.

It should be noted that the preceding comments about the nature of relationships refer specifically to individual experiences of leisure. Questions about the relationships between leisure service providers – that is, public and private organizations that deliver leisure services – have generally been kept separate from questions about the personal experience of leisure in traditional leisure research. A structural perspective about leisure challenges this separation, proposing that personal experiences of leisure are often mediated by institutionalized relationships between and among leisure providers. The relations among leisure providers are likely to be exchange relations, and subject to different theoretical concerns than those considered in research about personal leisure experiences. The organizational structures of leisure provision, however, will be considered again in later chapters of this volume, and particularly in Chapter 6.

Social networks

The importance of studying relationships is evidenced by the fact that relationships of significance (for example, those with meaningful affective and emotional bonds) are usually repetitive and relatively persistent, not random. That is, people generally like to see their friends and families, so they take action to visit, talk, and do activities together, rather than waiting for chance to structure encounters. Because such relationships are repetitive, they can be mapped and described on the basis of their characteristics, and studied using structural analytic methods.

The purpose of structural research is to analyze social relationships in juxta-position across systems. Social relationships are micro-level arrangements between people that also provide bridges to broader macro-level social structures. Considered simply from the perspective of size, relationships are the building blocks of larger social formations such as families, organizations, communities, social movements, or nations. Relative to specific, individual relationships, all of these levels of social order are larger in numbers of participants, more complex in arrangement, and potentially more persistent over time.

The arrangement or patterning of relationships across social space can be described as a 'social network.' The idea of a social network refers to structured arrangements of relationships across systems of people. Network analysis is a set of procedures for mapping and analyzing the multiple, simultaneous, extended interpersonal relationships of a set of actors all at once, and for analyzing the structural patterns and regularities which compose this network of relationships. Researchers hypothesize that variations in the patterns of relationships surrounding social actors affect the behavior of the actors and, correspondingly, social actors consciously manipulate situations in an effort to create desired structures (Leinhardt, 1977). A more complete review of social networks literature and relevant research issues is presented in Chapter 5.

The theoretical basis for a structural sociology of leisure is that social relationships form the basic elements of social network structures. It is only through understanding the actual patterning of relations among actors that researchers can uncover the socially constructed knowledge and realities that actors produce in interaction processes. Interpretations of the structures of social meanings, authority rules, systems of resource distribution, social knowledge, and other social and cultural features can only proceed with tangible referents to the social relationships through which reality is produced.

Community-based leisure networks
If leisure researchers study only the immediate social ties of primary groups that form the basis of leisure behavior, they run the risk of missing important structural patterns of social interaction, and they may misunderstand how and why specific relationships are chosen for leisure purposes. In this respect, the web of all social relationships surrounding particular social actors, not just the primary group relationships of close family and friends, should be of interest to researchers. The macro-level structures of relationships, meanings, and behaviors, composed of micro-level relational patterns of people involved in specific leisure pursuits, may provide researchers with information about the significance of leisure across society.

Given the informal, affective, weakly organized features of leisure behavior, it may be hypothesized that the proper social structural context of leisure should be that of community. Communities are collectivities containing various sets of strong and weak social ties, and other sets of as-yet-unknown and potential social ties, surrounding actors. From the range of all community members, leisure groupings and partnerships are derived and become visible at the level of participation. Leisure groupings are, therefore, not fixed, but flexible arrangements of people whose gathering is influenced by structural features of extended community environments. Moreover, others in communities are themselves connected (beyond ties to ego) in various ways, creating further possibilities for future group involvements. Leisure group participarion is just one subset of all the possible configurations formed by members of communities.

It should be acknowledged that there are many perspectives on the nature of 'community'. Communities may be defined as systems of interrelated activities, as geographic places, as common life-styles, as groups of people, and as centers of affiliation (Warren and Lyon, 1988). Summarizing academic literature, Lyon (1987: 5) reports that most definitions of community have 'the common elements of area, common ties, and social interaction.' Cohen (1985: 118) adds to this the idea that communities are symbolic constructions, too: 'People construct community symbolically, making it a resource and repository of meaning, and a referent of their identity.' The manifestations of community are seen in the structural patterns formed by 'a network of social relation[ships] marked by mutuality and emotional bonds' (Bender, 1978: 7).

The location of leisure choices and behaviors within the context of community provides a more comprehensive, structural approach to such disciplinary issues as the origin of social groups, the creation of leisure meanings, the development of personal identity, and the social constraints on behaviors. Analyzing the community basis of leisure establishes a link between the micro-level performances of leisure and the macro-level structuring of society. Under this theoretical orientation, earlier leisure research about primary groups of family and friends, social collectivities, and the social worlds of leisure can be reconceptualized as the formation of activity-specific clusters of people arranged within structured networks of relationships within extended communities of people.

Conducted within the context of social networks of community, leisure research would formalize hypotheses about the effects of networks of community relationships on leisure behavior and, reciprocally, about the abilities of social actors involved in leisure to skillfully manage or manipulate structures of community relationships. Why some community relationships, rather than others, are activated for leisure is one important research question. Others include queries about the processes by which multiple social relationships are arranged and ordered, and analyses of how relational networks are either intentionally structured (by people who intend consequences and who believe their actions have meaning), or unintentionally structured (as an outcome of collective social interaction, or the product of sometimes conflicting personal interests). Further, this approach raises equally interesting questions about how interpersonal relationships activated for leisure extend back into other community contexts of social involvement after leisure activities have concluded.

Under this approach, the experience of leisure is achieved in a social context characterized by the patterning of affective, voluntary, noninstrumental relationships within social networks of community. When such relationships are activated for leisure, they provide the structure, order, and coherence for recreation activity participation and for the social creation of leisure meanings. Conducted under intentions of personal choice, these relationships are also subject to the influence of structured relations among leisure service providers. In sum, relational and structural domains of leisure cannot be separated. Leisure experiences on personal levels are mediated by structural arrangements of leisure opportunity on broader structural levels.

To this point the emphasis has been on individual experiences of leisure. Considered in the aggregate, though, the leisure behaviors and relationships of many individuals across communities of people form extended structural patterns of social behaviors and meanings. These patterns reinforce and standardize the individual practices of leisure across society. The process of institutionalization is facilitated by the formal and informal organization of leisure services, facilities, settings, and resources. The social significance of leisure is not only in the arrangement of relational networks of personal leisure experience but also in the instrumental relationships forming the production networks of leisure provision.

Tourism provides a case in point. In the context of tourism, relationships assume many forms. Community leaders negotiate with resort developers, tourism businesses compete across markets, potential travelers consult tourism agencies, hosts serve guests, tourists meet other tourists, and so on. In broadest terms, tourism relations occur at many levels of social organization (Dann and Cohen, 1991) but, in practice, most of the research about relationships within tourism systems focuses on the micro levels of behavior, where tourists encounter other tourists or community 'locals' (Nash, 1981; Cohen, 1984; Nash and Smith, 1991).

The structural configuration of tourism provision, and the conventions of tourism in society, however, constrain as well as define the potential for individuals to enjoy tourism experiences. While both transitory and enduring relationships provide information, companionship, and resources that allow tourists to create and share meaningful experiences, it is the structured relationships among tourist providers that creates even initial interaction possibilities. Individual behaviors are at least partially structured by the system of relationships formalized by the industry and by social convention. The restrictions on travel made by the government of the former Soviet Union, implemented by tourist agencies, is one example of how structured networks affected the potential for individual tourism behavior. Another example is seen in the loosely organized relationships between natural resource agencies and local tourism providers, discussed by Selin and Beason (1991), the

Table 4.2 Research approaches in leisure sociology

	Level of Analysis	Social theories	Methods
Traditional sociology of leisure	Aggregated individuals	Stratification; limited socio-psychological	Survey; aggregation and quantitative analysis
Interpretive sociology of leisure	Relations between actors in groups and collectives	Symbolic interactionism; phenomenology; critical theory	Ethnographic; qualitative analysis
Structural sociology of leisure	Action and structure; micro–macro linkages	Interactionism; structuration processes; systems theory	Qualitative and quantitative; data analysis varies by level

incompleteness of which may result in an ineffective tourism delivery system mediating potential individual experiences. These authors assert that 'lack of awareness and differing ideologies act as barriers to effective communication between natural resource management agencies and tourism advocacy organizations' (p. 649). To what extent individual experiences are dampened or enhanced by structural arrangements (or lack thereof) beyond direct, personal control, remains an unresolved research issue.

Discussion: Structural Perspectives in Leisure

This volume provides a reinterpretation of leisure in structural terms. Missing from current leisure research is an understanding of how the experiences of leisure are socially constructed realities developing within the interpersonal relationships of daily life. Such relationships are the source of leisure behaviors and meanings, and are patterned in extended network structures across society. The institutionalization of leisure occurs on three levels: at the individual level, where leisure is experienced; in the context of community, where individuals stand in relation to diverse sets of others; and across society, where leisure services are provided. It is the interplay of multiple levels of social order, and multiple processes of social organization, that provides structure to leisure behaviors and meanings.

Table 4.2 compares traditional and interpretive approaches with structural approaches in the sociology of leisure. Traditional models in leisure ignore the relationships among people in larger social networks of community, and the influence of these networks on action and meaning in leisure. But people do not suddenly appear onsite at leisure or recreation places without some prior social involvements or understandings guiding their choices; they live in worlds of potentially expansive and diverse social connections. Leisure is more than simply an individual or small-group experience, mediated at times by organizations, agencies, or businesses that provide leisure services. Leisure behaviors and meanings are constrained, and also facilitated, by the types of relational structures in which people are involved during daily community life. Sociological thinking about leisure should be concerned with how the broad range of community social contacts and relationships surrounding individuals might encourage or prohibit leisure opportunities. A structural sociology of leisure raises these kinds of issues.

There are two fundamental issues critical to the development of a structural sociology of leisure. First, individuals have the potential for involvement in a wide variety of social ties. As they progress through life, personal characteristics, residential locale, interests, work, social situation, and other factors provide opportunities to participate in social communities and to foster relationships of various kinds. The entire pattern of social relationships surrounding individuals, especially those that are activated for leisure purposes, should be the focus of a structural sociology of leisure.

A second fundamental issue in a structural sociology of leisure concerns the institutionalization of relationships across society. From the standpoint of an individual, extended patterns of relationships on a societal level are largely invisible. That does not imply, however, that they have little importance. Markets are abstract, but are certainly not neutral (Kelly, 1992). Likewise, religions, job opportunities, and academic colleagues are structurally diffuse, but the relations between members have consequences for individual behaviors. Sociologists should be concerned with the structuring and influence of leisure networks (both personal and organizational) across society, and the implications of these patterns for individual-level choices and actions.

These two structural considerations rarely meet in traditional and interpretive research about leisure sociology. Analyses conducted on the micro level focus on individuals, their characteristics, and their involvements in small-group settings. The few studies conducted at the macro level evaluate societal demographic and socioeconomic conditions or national time-use patterns, and infer consequences for individual leisure consumers. However, the definition of social structures as relatively predictable patterns of human relationships and interactions across society centers attention on the location of relationships within structures, and calls for theories and methods that merge levels of analysis. The intersection of social relationships with social structures is best studied under a network analytic approach.

The structural perspective promoted in this book does not deny the importance of previous conceptualizations of leisure (feeling, activity, time) but does recast them as outcomes of patterned interpersonal relationships. That is, leisure feelings, expressed in activities undertaken during free time, are assumed to arise as a result of the structuring processes of personal involvement with other people in society. Personal meanings and behaviors related to leisure become 'social' in the context of structured relationships and interactions with others. These patterns of involvement are themselves institutionalized as socially constructed meanings and organized patterns of behavior. Seen from the standpoint of society, rather than from the perspective of individuals or small groups, these interaction patterns form extended networks of social ties that both constrain as well as facilitate the behaviors of the actors involved.

Structural research about leisure requires both micro-level analyses of relevant social interactions within interpersonal relationships and macro-level analyses of the social network structures that contain leisure relationships. Any number of theories may appropriately link these levels of analysis. For example, some researchers might wish to study the social construction of leisure reality, hypothesizing about the interactionist features of relationships and the structural features of networks that facilitate the transmission of social meanings. Other researchers might be interested in how the exchange of information or resources across network subgroups enhances leisure opportunity on the personal level.

Benefits of a structural sociology of leisure

Structural sociology presents a new perspective and broader alternatives for analyzing the social significance of leisure. There are at least three categories of research that should receive renewed attention under a structural perspective. These include: (1) research about the onsite, activity-centered groupings of leisure behavior, with the goal of providing a more complete understanding of the structural conditions that influence how and why particular types of social groupings form and persist across recreation places; (2) research about the community basis of leisure, in which networks of community relationships are evaluated for their contributions to the groupings of individuals and collectivities at leisure places; and (3) research about how relationships activated for leisure become institutionalized across society, and potentially influence future community network ties, either by direct relational interactions between persons or by the creation of new social meanings about leisure.

There are several benefits to analyzing leisure in structural terms. First, relationships have past, present, and future dimensions. A structural approach begins to question how past relational commitments influence current and even future leisure choices. Additionally, the specification of relational types and contents that emerge in leisure contexts may help clarify distinctions between leisure and other domains of community involvement. Under what structural conditions might relations of the workplace, or school, or religious affiliation, become transformed for leisure? How are social networks affected when relational contents overlap? Further, the structural perspective allows researchers to center leisure meanings and intentions in the processes of interaction emerging from social relationships. This removes the psychological reductionism from leisure research, and creates opportunities for analyses of basic communication processes that foster leisure behavior.

The consequences of variable relational patterns across community networks for individual behavior and the success of individual attempts to structure relations in the social environment are topics that have rarely been addressed in traditional leisure research. In the remaining chapters, basic approaches in structural theorizing and social network analysis are reviewed, the current status of research about leisure networks is evaluated, and future research considerations in the structural analysis of leisure are discussed.

5

Social networks research

Socialization always takes place in the context of a specific social structure. Not only its contents but also its measure of 'success' have social-structural conditions and social-structural consequences. In other words, the micro-sociological or social-psychological analysis of phenomena of internalization must always have as its background a macro-sociological understanding of their structural aspects.

(Berger and Luckmann, 1966: 163)

Introduction

Models of leisure that gave primacy to social groups and life cycle effects focused attention on the interactions of individuals engaged in small, primary group relationships. But the world is not only reducible to individuals or groups. Groups are made up of people, who have simultaneous social commitments and broader involvements in society. Individuals and social groups should be conceived as elements of larger community social networks.

The traditional sociological approach to analyzing dyadic and small-group interactions focuses on how attributes of individuals (for example, age, occupation, and social status) contribute to normative or functional explanations of social behavior (McCord, 1980). Wellman (1988: 31) comments that 'Mainstream sociological studies treat social structure and process as the sum of individual actors' personal attributes . . . lumped into social categories [and] aggregate profiles.' Alternatively, more recent approaches from the perspective of structural sociology elevate an actor's participation in social relationships to the forefront of research attention, looking to relational attributes as primary explanations of structural patterns.

Under these new approaches, social 'structure' refers to the patterning and distribution of significant relationships across society. Emerging social network models propose that social structure 'is best understood in terms of a dynamic interplay between the *relations* between and among persons . . . and the *positions* and *roles* they occupy within a social system' (Berkowitz, 1982: 3). He later explains, '[If] the credo of conventional social science is "categories have consequences," the structuralist rebuttal would be "consequences have categories," that is, patterns of relations among members of sets of elements produce or yield those social entities which we recognize and interpret as social groups' (p. 14).

There is no ascending natural order of social groupings in a network, and no single encompassing structural theory that guides research about networks. Rather, the key issue is 'how the relations are arranged [and] how the behavior of individuals depends on their location in this arrangement' (Leinhardt, 1977: xiii). Variability in network structures is hypothesized to be related to the behavior of social actors. Additionally, the intentions and abilities of social actors to skillfully influence relational situations are assumed to affect the patterning of network structures. The purpose of this chapter is to present an overview of social networks thinking and writing as it details significant issues, concepts, and research findings. For illustrative purposes, a model of a hypothetical social network among 30 friends and friends-of-friends is given in Figure 5.1.

Operationalizing Structure

Social network models are markedly different from earlier, more traditional sociological approaches to the study of social structure. Berkowitz (1982: 3) described the structuralist position in the following manner:

> Rather than beginning with an a priori classification of the observable world into a discrete set of categories, [structuralists] postulated the opposite: begin with a set of relations and from them derive a typology and map of the structure of groups.

In this way, social structure is treated as 'a network of networks that may or may not be partitioned into discrete groups' (Wellman, 1988: 20). Social relationships are the basic units of analysis, and a 'network' itself is defined as 'a specific set of linkages among a defined set of persons' (Mitchell, 1969: 2). Network scholars propose that people conduct their daily affairs as members of social networks, that they intentionally manipulate network ties for personal benefit, and that social structures also exert influence on individual behavior in society.

The idea of a network, or web of relationships, became useful when traditional approaches to studying bounded groups in society failed to describe adequately the reality of relational ties among people. For example, Bott (1971: 313) said of her London research families,

> [They] did not live in groups. They 'lived' in networks, if one can use the term 'lived in' to describe the situation of being in contact with a set of people and organizations, some of whom were in contact with one another and some of whom were not.

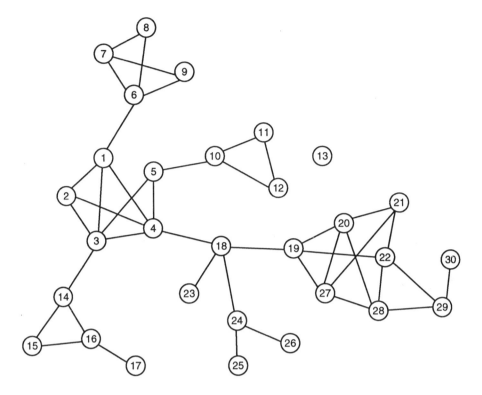

Figure 5.1 Hypothetical social network for a system of 30 actors

Though social networks may be invisible even to the participants related within the structures, researchers believe that networks exert influence directly and indirectly on social behavior.

The network perspective reformulates the basic principles of traditional sociological theorizing. Summarizing developments in the networks paradigm, Wellman (1988: 20) described five basic assumptions of the new approach to structural inquiry. These are: (1) the world is composed of networks, not groups; (2) social structures determine the operation of dyadic relationships; (3) structured social relationships are a more powerful source of sociological explanation than personal attributes of system members; (4) norms emerge from location in structured systems of social relationships; and (5) structural methods supplement and supplant individualistic methods.

The strength of the network approach to structural analysis is in analyzing what Wellman (1988: 33) calls 'the social distribution of possibilities.' Social relationships are not always symmetrical, not always voluntarily chosen, and sometimes not even reciprocal. People have differential access to information, resources, power, or other benefits (Wellman and Berkowitz, 1988b) through relationships, and correspondingly different opportunities for participation in society. The study of social networks encourages researchers to analyze patterns of social relationships within social structures, and therefore to account for social behaviors on both micro and macro levels. Marsden and Lin (1982: 10) sum up the utility of the network approach to social structure as follows:

> The network orientation offers new approaches to describing and studying social structure and to dealing with the complex problem of integrating levels of analysis: the manner in which individual actions create social structure; the manner in which social structure, once created, constrains individual and collective action; or the manner in which attitudes and behaviors of actors are determined by the social context in which action takes place.

The Development of Networks Thinking

The networks idea arose simultaneously in a number of different scientific disciplines. For example, in biology and physics, the network metaphor was utilized to describe 'chains' or 'webs' of cellular and molecular interactions (von Bertalanffy, 1950). In wildlife biology and population ecology, network applications were used to describe the movement of animal herds across land areas during seasonal migrations (Lewis, 1977). Other researchers have applied network concepts to transportation analysis (Glover and Rogozinski, 1982).

In the social sciences, networks research developed after World War II as a way for sociologists, anthropologists, and social psychologists to describe and analyze the consequences of relational ties among people in small groups, organizations, and tribal and village communities (Simmel, 1950; Moreno, 1951; Barnes, 1954; Bott, 1955; Boissevain, 1974). Rogers (1987: 287) comments that 'Sociometry was the direct ancestor of today's social network analysis . . . [and] the second coming of network analysis began [with] the invasion of social science by computers.'

The earlier scientific tradition of sociometric research was extended beyond small-group settings in two ways. First, sociometric analysis was formalized to attach descriptive names to different patterns of relationships in groups. Leinhardt (1977: xiv) said, 'Moreno gave names . . . to various features of sociometric data. . . . "Stars", for example, were what he called highly chosen individuals, and "isolates" were those rarely chosen.'

Second, mathematical sociologists began to study the algebraic properties of social networks, and to model the structural transformations that occurred with changes in network size and connectivity (Heider, 1946/1977; Harary, 1959/1977; Davis, 1967; Lorrain and White, 1971). With the improvement of computer analysis techniques in the 1970s, network analysis became an established field of inquiry. Mitchell (1969), Leinhardt (1977), Tichy *et al.* (1979), and Rogers (1987) provide comprehensive reviews of the history of networks thinking in social research.

The vision of a network of people connected through relational ties is more than simply a metaphor. Network analysis is a set of methods for mapping the real, often simultaneous, interpersonal relationships and interactions among a set of social actors, and then analyzing how structural regularities influence the behavior of the actors (Mitchell, 1969; Bott, 1971; Barnes, 1972; Leinhardt, 1977; Rogers and Kincaid, 1981; Marsden and Lin, 1982; Wellman and Berkowitz, 1988b). Social actors are 'nodes' in the network, and the ties between them are called 'links.' For example, in Figure 5.1, the actors (nodes) are identified by circled numbers, while the links are illustrated by lines connecting the nodes. The resulting network map, displaying a composite pattern of actual relations that exist among a defined set of nodes, is used to answer questions and introduce and examine hypotheses about the patterning of social relationships across social structures.

Social network analysis provides an empirical approach that links interactionist and structural considerations in the analysis of social behavior. Researchers have used network approaches to map actual and potential communication linkages, exchange relations, kinship systems, ties of sentiment, power and influence relations, and policy structures, among people. The networks perspective encompasses a variety of theoretical applications, and, as Price (1981: 283) remarks, 'network studies [currently] constitute a very disparate collection of enquiries made from divergent theoretical standpoints.'

In the social sciences, network analysis techniques have been applied to study issues at various levels of social organization, including the meaning of extended social ties for community cohesion and involvement, personal health and well-being, social exchange (such as helping behavior and job-seeking assistance), and organizational effectiveness. The approach is a powerful tool for mapping extended relationships between people, for analyzing the effects of relationships on structures, and for understanding how social structures constrain as well as facilitate interaction and opportunity.

Types of networks

In the social sciences, the networks model has seen various applications. The earliest network studies were of 'egocentric networks' (the personal ties surrounding an individual actor) within the context of a bounded collectivity (such as a family, tribe, or remote community). Bott (1971: 320) defined egocentric networks as 'all or some of the social units (individuals or groups) with whom a particular individual or group is in contact.' Egocentric network studies begin with the social actor and focus on the structuring of multiple personal relationships surrounding that person or collectivity (Bott, 1971; Jones and Fischer, 1978).

Some social networks researchers are not interested in the multiple egocentric ties of specific social actors, but in the exact paths of directed linkages between persons. Some examples of this tradition in the study of social networks are seen in small-world studies (Travers and Milgram, 1969), diffusion of innovations research (Coleman *et al.*, 1957), and studies of communication linkages and resource transfers that support productivity within organizations or communities. In these studies it is critical to specify the content of the relationships under study, since the activation of ties may depend on the context.

More recently, researchers have become involved in ambitious projects to model 'networks of networks,' where network patterns are not necessarily stable or consistent over time (Doreian, 1986; Wellman and Berkowitz, 1988b). In this research, emphasis is on the clustering of subgroups within networks, and in analysis of how these intersect with clusterings in other networks. Social actors are seen as being enmeshed in multiple networks all at once, and as having varying commitments and responsibilities within a multitude of relational ties.

The nature of relationships

A key conceptual issue in studying social networks is defining the types of relational ties that are the focus of research. This is an issue of more than passing interest: the lack of a theory of relationships results in an inability to describe the criteria upon which social structure is assumed to develop. Rules of inclusion are important because, in practice, it is almost impossible to account for every social tie in an actor's environment. The specification of relational theories of interest should precede any network analysis.

This is not a trivial issue. In research about ties of sociability, for example, a weighting process may be needed to differentiate among types of relationships. Do daily greetings to the mailman have the same weight as sociable chatter with a colleague, or long-distance phone conversations with a best friend? Networks models, in themselves, provide no standard for determining where relationships begin and end, or which inclusion rules are to be used in different circumstances. Thus it is important that theoretical approaches are well described to avoid overstating or undervaluing the importance of specific social ties. As Jones and Fischer (1978: 39) commented, 'We suspect [that] . . . conclusions about people's whole social world are often inaccurately generalized from data on narrowly defined sets of relations.'

The imperative for networks researchers, then, is to 'elaborate a theoretical framework and methodological protocol to specify which relations in what temporal and social context are to be regarded as the focus of attention' (Price, 1981: 284). This exercise will also help define the boundaries of the network system under study. The boundary issue remains hazy: since the size and composition of social networks are not specified, but determined through research, it is up to the researcher to identify clearly the relations under study and the ways in which they are theoretically relevant.

Table 5.1 Social network measures

Type	Definition
Interactional criteria	
1. Frequency of communication	Number and continuity of interactions over time
2. Content of ties	Purpose and functions of relation; types of relational tie (exchange, obligation, sentiment, power)
3. Multiplexity	Redundancy of relationships: number of contents combined in a relationship
4. Reciprocity	Degree of symmetry in relation (if A chooses B, does B choose A?)
5. Strength of ties (strong, weak)	Relative measure of time, affect, intensity, mutuality
Structural criteria	
1. Size	Number of people or relations in network
2. Density	Connectedness of network; actual links computed as proportion of total links
3. Distance or proximity	Number of links between any two nodes in network
4. Centrality	Adjacency and influence of nodes and subgroups in network
5. Clustering	Partition of ties into network subgroups and cliques
6. Network roles:	
(a) Isolate	Peripheral node in a network
(b) Bridge	Group member who provides a link to another network subgroup
(c) Liaison	Node that links several groups without being a member of any group
(d) Star	Node with largest number of communication links

Reprinted with permission from *Leisure Sciences* **12** (3), 251–63.

Network sampling

Regardless of the type of network under study (personal egocentric networks, extended chains of relations within or across networks, or networks of networks), the data to be collected are sociometric in nature. Questions are asked about a social actor's interpersonal relationships, exchanges, and communication with other relevant social actors. Typical topics include identifying the list of people linked in certain types of relationships to ego, describing the types of relationships between ego and an other, exploring how strongly or weakly ego is connected to an other, or analyzing how frequently ego and an other are in contact, the means by which ego and an other stay in contact, and the activities they share. Table 5.1 details some of the interactional criteria used to evaluate social relationships in networks. Interactional criteria include: the frequency of communication between actors; the type and content of the relationship (exchange, kinship, sentiment); whether ties are reciprocal between actors; and the extent to which ties are intense and durable.

Network data are traditionally gathered using observational and interview techniques (when a limited number of ties are being considered), or question-naire methods (when all network members can be contacted within bounded settings, such as organizations or isolated communities). However, data col-lection is labor-intensive for researchers, and requires a high degree of recall accuracy from subjects. Moreover, Barnes (1972: 24) notes that these methods provide a researcher with data about only immediate contacts of the subject 'forgetting about – because he does not know about – the other [social] relations impinging on these individuals.'

Not the least of the data collection and analysis problems in social networks research is understanding what people mean by the relational terms they use. Social actors assign meanings to interpersonal relations based on a variety of criteria. For example, to some people, an 'immediate family member' may also be considered a 'best friend,' and reported as such in a name-eliciting question. Yet other people may distinguish between friends and kin without overlapping affect with roles. Jones and Fischer (1978: 4) found that '[Subjects] have sur-prisingly poor recall of the people they know,' and, furthermore, 'Respondents [sometimes] pad their lists of relations with people who do not fit the descrip-tion given [in order not to appear unpopular or unloved].'

Measuring network structure

When a map of a social network is drawn, the linkages refer to sometimes-utilized, conditional channels of communication, and to relational ties that have specific kinds of contents. In social research, a network map should be conceived as a picture of probabilistic ties (links) among entities (nodes) at a given point in time, where the situation or context has encouraged network members to invest social relationships with meaning.

Networks research analyzes significant features of social relationships and the extended structures in which relationships are contained (Mitchell, 1969; Barnes, 1972). In addition to the interactional criteria previously mentioned, a description of structural criteria used in analyzing networks is also presented in Table 5.1. Structural measures of networks include: the size of the network; network density (whether there are many or few linkages throughout the network); and clusterability (the extent to which the entire network can be partitioned into smaller groups and cliques).

While these and other criteria are important elements of social structure, there is little consensus in the literature concerning which criteria to select for different circumstances, and even less consensus about how to operationalize the chosen variables. For example, a theory of helping behavior may suggest that the density of a person's social network contributes to specific behavioral outcomes, such as giving more or less help when other network members are aware that help has been requested. However, the concept of 'density' has been used in a variety of different ways in networks research, and it is not always entirely clear which approach is appropriate under what conditions (Turner, 1967; Barnes, 1969; Bott, 1971; Price, 1981).

Network clusters and subgroups

Patterns of relational linkages surrounding actors in a network structure can be described using a variety of approaches. Well-connected individuals might be described as 'stars,' and those who are in positions on the boundary or peripheral to the network are called 'isolates.' Terms such as 'gatekeepers,' 'bridges,' and 'liaisons' have been used to describe communication roles in a network (Rogers and Kincaid, 1981; see also Table 5.1). These terms all refer to patterns of social ties surrounding an individual, and theoretical questions can be raised about how these structural patterns influence that particular person's behavior.

One might also be interested in aggregating data within sections of a network and in comparing networks across settings. In this case, it is desirable to analyze the ways in which a complete network can be partitioned into subgroups (also called 'cliques' or 'clusters') containing similar network members, and excluding those who have different sets of social ties. Two approaches to subdividing networks are common: the relational approach and the positional approach.

Relational and positional approaches can be distinguished from one another by the theories which support them, and the network subgroups which they create. Burt (1978: 189) says, 'The relational approach, developing from traditional sociometry, focuses on relations between actors . . . and aggregates actors connected by cohesive bonds into "cliques".' That is, in any social network, there will be 'areas' of the network where social relations are more dense (i.e., actors are connected to one another more strongly than they are connected to others). These relations appear to form subgroups in the network of relations.

One the other hand, the positional approach 'focuses on the patterns of relations in which an actor is involved, and aggregates actors with similar patterns . . . into jointly occupied positions' (*ibid.*). Persons who occupy these positions are called 'structurally equivalent actors.' These actors do not necessarily have similar kinds (contents) of social relations, but they have similar patterns of relationships with others in the network. For example, two isolated persons may lack social ties to others and so be considered structurally equivalent, whether or not they share a relationship with one another.

It is clear that the relational and positional approaches may yield different subgroups in analyzing social networks. Which approach one chooses to use in network analysis depends on the assumptions and goals of the research. Blau (1982: 277) outlines the dilemma in the following manner: 'Do we first analyze social relations and distinguish positions on the basis of differences in patterns of relations, or do we start by categorizing people by social positions to examine the patterns of relations among them?' Both approaches may be used for comparative purposes and for validating network structures (Burt, 1976, 1978, 1980; Blau, 1981, 1982; Rogers, 1987).

Benefits of networks research

For purposes of illustration, some of the structural criteria of Table 5.1 can be described using the previously presented Figure 5.1. (Without knowing anything about the interactional criteria on which Figure 5.1 was based, it is nearly impossible to determine criteria such as frequency, reciprocity, or strength of ties.) The size of the network is 30 members. If all network members were equally and fully connected to one another, the network would be considered very dense. In fact, though, the members are not entirely connected, and the density of the network could be calculated by expressing the actual number of linkages as a proportion of the total number of possible network linkages. The specific formulas for determining possible network density and actual network density are presented by Berkowitz (1982: 46):

A. *Maximum network density*:

$$\frac{N(N-1)}{2}$$

(where N = number of nodes).

B. *Actual network density*:

$$\frac{a}{\dfrac{N(N-1)}{2}} = \frac{2a}{N(N-1)}$$

(where N = number of nodes; a = number of actual ties).

In Figure 5.1 the number of nodes is 30; the actual number of ties is 42; and the density percentage is 9.65 percent (after multiplying the solution of formula B by 100). Given that maximum network density refers to the possibility that all nodes are in contact with one another, it is clear that Figure 5.1 has very low density.

Distance measures for Figure 5.1 could also be computed by evaluating the proximity of nodes to one another. For example, the shortest distance between nodes 1 and 29 is five links; but nodes 1 and 3 are in immediate contact, and nodes 1 and 9 are linked by only one other intermediary. Structural theory holds that the distance between members of a network affects, among other things, communication potential, transfer of resources, and ability to exert power.

Figure 5.1 also shows that some of the members of the network are more central than others, and that the network can be partitioned into subgroups comprising select members. The nodes 1, 2, 3, 4, and 5 form a group, as do members 10, 11, and 12. Altogether, there are five groups evident in this network, although the largest group (on the right of the diagram, including member 22) is considerably more complex than some of the others. Network roles can also be identified in Figure 5.1: for example, member 13 is a true isolate, while members 17, 23, 25, 26, and 30 are semi-isolates or peripheral network members (each has only one tie to another in the network). Member 18 is a liaison, and the bridges are members 1, 3, 5, 6, 10, and 14. A number of network members have four links with others in the network, but the stars in this network would be members 3 and 4, who each have five ties. Comparing the structure of this network with that of other networks (or making comparisons of the same network over time) may lead to new insights about the nature of particular behaviors under study (such as leisure behaviors).

There are a number of potential benefits to the networks approach for analysis of social structure. First, network analysis provides a visual map and picture of how defined sets of social actors stand in relation to one another based on specific interaction criteria. Some of the computer programs used to analyze network data produce two- or three-dimensional network structure maps illustrating the relative location of actors in social space and the relations which link them together (see, for example, the description of the NEGOPY program by Richards and Rice, 1981). Second, as a result of advances in computer technology, different kinds of relational contents can be mapped over one another in network representations, providing a more comprehensive picture of the intensity and extensity of a field of social relations.

Third, network data are gathered using sociometric-type questions, which have the benefit of being easily understandable for subjects, and 'real' in their experience. While there are significant problems in estimation of numbers of linkages, and often in recall of interactions by respondents, these network data provide for a researcher a wealth and richness of information on which to base analyses of social structure.

Fourth, the measures of distance, proximity, or similarity across networks are developed from evidence of everyday, observable behavior in social relationships. For example, if person A talks with person B every day, but talks with person C only once a year, we might hypothesize that persons A and B are 'closer' friends with respect to some defined criteria. Finally, the network approach provides analyses of individual linkages between pairs of actors, as well as analyses of substructures (groups, clusters, cliques) within the network system under study. Questions about the influence of structure on individual behavior, and the ability of actors to influence social structure, are answered with reference to the patterning of relationships across social networks.

Social Networks Research: An Overview

Social networks research has grown rapidly over the past two decades. A scholarly journal, *Social Networks*, begun in 1978, provides a forum for research, and a professional society dedicated to the study of social networks (the International Network for Social Network Analysis, INSNA) arranges yearly conferences to discuss networks issues. INSNA also produces a bulletin called *Connections* to keep networks researchers informed about events, research developments, and the activities of other scholars. Networks research is also becoming more popular in mainstream social science disciplines, and scholarly articles dealing with networks topics are appearing in a variety of disciplinary journals.

Given the impossibility of discussing the entire body of published research work that addresses networks issues, this section will discuss only a small segment of literature that is likely to have particular relevance for leisure research. The primary groups focus of theoretical traditions in the sociology of leisure suggests that the networks literature likely to be most transferable is research conducted from the perspective of relational (rather than positional) social networks. Relational networks are structures of ties among individuals based on close, intimate, personal connections and associations. This extensive literature includes research about family interactions, friendship formation, acquaintance networks, extended ties of sociability across communities, and methodological issues in networks research.

Though the entire body of networks research includes a variety of other theoretical perspectives and topics (for example, analyses of corporate or organizational network structures, interorganizational networks, resource exchanges, or mathematical modeling of networks), these topics are seen as peripheral to understanding the creation and institutionalization of leisure behavior in society, and will not be reviewed here. In the remainder of this chapter, networks research conducted by sociologists and anthropologists will be presented; in the next chapter, social networks research conducted by leisure and recreation scholars will be highlighted.

Introductory and reference papers

Several seminal papers guided development of the social networks idea in sociology and anthropology. These papers contain meticulous discussions of the history, concepts and issues, methodological techniques, and status of networks research as social science, and are useful introductions to the key ideas of networks thinking and to subsequent applications of the networks idea in empirical research.

From anthropological perspectives, Mitchell (1969) reviewed historical uses of the term 'network' and described in detail the morphological and interactional criteria used in network analysis. Bott (1971) and Barnes (1972) provided comprehensive reviews of early theoretical and empirical research about social networks, focusing specifically on applications in family and small community settings. There are also a number of important collections of theoretical and empirical writings about social networks produced by sociologists. These include three edited volumes (Leinhardt, 1977; Marsden and

Lin, 1982; Burt and Minor, 1983) discussing early formulations and applications of the networks idea in social research. In addition, a text (Berkowitz, 1982) and a more recent set of papers (Wellman and Berkowitz, 1988b), develop the networks idea considerably and extend methods more broadly in discussing issues of social structure.

In addition to these sources, there are occasional state-of-the-field reviews (Rogers, 1987) and also pertinent writings from other disciplines. For example, communication theories provide the basis for network analysis in Rogers and Kincaid's (1981) book *Communication Networks*, and Tichy *et al.* (1979) describe networks applications for analyses of complex organizations. A comprehensive guide for researchers conducting and analyzing social networks is a small book entitled simply *Network Analysis* (Knoke and Kuklinski, 1982).

Research on primary and extended relationships

The network model has been used in sociology to study a variety of theoretical issues concerning primary and extended relationships, including family roles, friendship formation, life satisfaction based on network involvements, and community cohesion. Much of the recent networks research on these topics has evolved from origins in sociological and anthropological community studies, and is inspired by several significant research projects. These include, among others, Barnes's (1954) study of kinship and friendship patterns in a Norwegian fishing village; Bott's (1955) study of the relational patterns of husbands and wives in London suburban families; a series of research studies conducted by Fischer and associates (Jones and Fischer, 1978; Fischer and Phillips, 1979; Fischer, 1982b) in California; Wellman's (1979) community studies in Toronto; and Granovetter's (1973) analyses of job-seeking behaviors among residents of a Boston suburb, and of social cohesion within ethnic communities of Boston.

Bott's (1955, 1971) work is especially interesting for leisure and recreation researchers. In her research about the daily work, family, and social habits of a set of London research families (including their leisure activities), she found that a traditional 'social class' study using standard socioeconomic variables failed to account adequately for variation in the way spouses performed family roles. Refocusing her study on the network relationships of the husbands and wives, Bott (1955: 349) found support for the hypothesis that 'the degree of segregation in the role-relationship of husband and wife varies directly with the connectedness of the family's social network.' That is, the more separate the roles of husbands and wives, the more connected the network, and vice versa. She used as one indicator of role relationship the amount of leisure time spouses spent together, suggesting a relation between free time and the degree of connectedness in social networks of spouses.

Bott's hypothesis about the importance of network connections for conjugal role performance has received mixed support from later researchers intrigued with her hypothesis (Udry and Hall, 1965; Turner, 1967; Lee, 1980; Richards, 1980; Rogler and Procidano, 1986; Yi, 1986). Leisure researchers, however, have apparently not explored her hypothesis in research about family leisure orientations, though it would seem to be a rich area for future work.

Bott had analyzed the ego-relationships of husbands and wives, seen against a backdrop of extended family and neighbor relations. Other sociologists have worked from the opposite direction: they begin with an analysis of community relations, and study either the structures of whole communities or the clusters and subgroups within them. For example, Litwak and Szelenyi (1969) and Wellman (1979) studied helping behavior among kin, friends, and acquaintances in large urban areas. Colfer and Colfer (1978) analyzed divisions between public- and private-sector employees living in a rural Washington State logging community. Johnson and Miller (1983) analyzed marginal members of Italian fishing groups in an Alaskan community. Freudenburg (1986) considered the structures and meanings of acquaintanceship patterns in an energy boom town.

An ambitious program of community network studies, analyzing egocentric relational patterns across a number of communities, was illustrated in the work of Fischer and colleagues on the Northern California Community Study, completed in 1977. Much of the empirical work from the Northern California study focuses on the nature of friendships and the influence of social network ties on people's sense of 'community' (Fischer, 1982a, b). One study reported on the consequences of being socially isolated (Fischer and Phillips, 1979); another discussed the importance of network ties as informal support systems for older people, especially women (Steuve and Fischer, 1978).

In both studies, social networks were seen as 'resources,' containing linkages that provided health care, information, companionship and emotional support, and exchange of material goods and services between people in communities. The conception of social networks as resources for social support, providing for the well-being and happiness of members, is further developed by Lin (1982) and by Campbell *et al.* (1986), and is also an emerging theme in the literature of social gerontology (Adams, 1987; Burt, 1987; Lawton and Moss, 1987; Mitchell, 1987; Milardo, 1988a). Conclusions from this research indicate that social well-being is related to the connectedness of personal networks surrounding individuals, and that people who have more network ties and stronger relationships are happier in life.

The structural and behavioral importance of friendships is an important question, and continues to spark the interest of researchers. Fischer (1982a: 306) proposed that 'there is something distinctive about the contents of relations which people called "friends". These ties [tend] primarily to be relations of sociability.' Hallinan (1978), Runger and Wasserman (1980), Matthews (1986), Moody (1986), and Milardo (1988a) present several approaches to the study of friendships through the life course. Their work raises questions about exactly which others are labelled as 'friends,' and what friend relationships mean in the context of all other social involvements.

One of the most frequently cited papers on the topic of networks as resources is Granovetter's (1973) article, 'The strength of weak ties' (see also Granovetter, 1982). In research about the social relationships among members of ethnic communities in Boston, and the ways in which people locate new jobs, Granovetter found important differences between strong and weak ties across social networks. He proposed that 'Weak ties are more likely to link members of *different* small groups than are strong ones, which tend to be concentrated within groups' (1973: 1376). As a result, weak ties provide connections between people who do not know one another well, thereby facilitating the transfer of new information, providing bridges between strongly connected groups of people, and contributing to community integration.

Friedkin (1980) found support for Granovetter's model in a test among work associates; however, Greenbaum (1982) reports mixed results for the model when applied in neighborhood social networks. The idea that weak and strong ties have different characteristics might be very useful in applications to leisure research. Traditional approaches to studying the qualities of primary groups in leisure behavior ignore possibilities that weak ties might also influence significant dimensions of the leisure experience.

The conception of relationships as social resources represents a preliminary formulation of an exchange theory of relationships in network structures. Wellman and Berkowitz (1988a) specifically focus on networks as structures of exchange relations, considering 'how relations structure resource allocation under conditions of scarcity and how these often asymmetrical relations concatenate into complex . . . networks of power and dependency' (p. 6). Whether friendship or kin relations can also be analyzed as social resources raises interesting questions about the overlap of contexts within relations.

Network methodology

Data collection procedures for social networks research are not unlike other methods of respondent contact in the social sciences, though analysis of data takes some unique forms. A common approach for collecting data on small egocentric networks is to employ ethnographic methods, including participant observation (Barnes, 1954) and personal interviewing (Bott, 1971; Wellman, 1979). Some researchers have had subjects use daily logs to record existing personal contacts (Conrath *et al.*, 1983) in an attempt to devise a sociometric census. Other researchers have traced linkages through 'snowball sampling' (Goodman, 1961) or in 'small world' studies (Milgram, 1967; Travers and Milgram, 1969). In both of these cases it is the chains of personal connections through society which are of interest to the researcher rather than all the personal contacts of individual subjects. Bernard *et al.* (1980), Romney and Weller (1984), Hammer (1984), and Sudman (1985) all consider the question of whether respondents are accurate in reporting their relational ties.

Another approach to collecting egocentric network data is by mass survey (including mail or personally administered questionnaires). Jones and Fischer (1978) describe the random sampling procedures used in the Northern California Community Study to obtain data about the core exchange-based networks of urbanites in several cities in northern California. Their report includes examples of questions administered in pilot and final versions of the study. Descriptions of the random sampling procedures used for large populations and networks are provided by Granovetter (1976), Frank (1978), Burt (1981), Erickson *et al.* (1981), and Erickson and Nosanchuk (1983).

Once networks are displayed, researchers attempt to answer questions about the patterning of relationships and subgroups across networks, and hypothesize about the influence of structure on behavior. The clustering of social actors within network subgroups is analyzed by van Poucke (1980), Wilson (1982), Hammer (1985), and Johnson and Miller (1986). Useful discussions of network connectivity and clustering methods are provided by Barnes (1969), Breiger (1974), Alba and Moore (1978), Burt (1976, 1978, 1980), Harary and Batell (1981), and Price (1981).

Summary

The purpose of describing the social network approach to structural analysis is to provide a foundation for the eventual application of network analytic techniques in leisure research. Since there are currently only a limited number of isolated attempts to apply network principles to leisure problems, this detailed review is necessary to provide a background in structural thinking for scholars who are not familiar with the networks approach. In the following chapter, applications of the networks idea in leisure research are reviewed and analyzed.

6

Social networks research in leisure

In sum, we must all have some sense that our private lives connect to the larger meanings of our social circles and our community's public life. A central function of leisure settings and services is to provide that necessary connection. We are all actors in a multiplicity of human dramas. We are children, parents, friends, neighbors and members of ethnic, cultural and national groupings. These are the raw material of our identities.

(Burch, 1986: V–87)

Introduction

When asked about their memorable travel experiences, people often say that their most vivid memories involved meeting and getting to know other people who lived in the places they were visiting. These relationships are highly valued because they provide personal glimpses into new places and cultures in a manner that makes the visitor a participant, not simply a tourist. While many tourists rely on fate or chance to influence their encounters, a few people actually plan in advance to meet others they do not know. One of the latter, a woman planning to visit India for a summer, 'created' the possibilities for memories through social relationships even before she left home. Her efforts are described in a travel article in a Denver, Colorado, metropolitan newspaper (Andrus, 1992). The author, Carol Andrus, reported (p. 1T)

> I knew no one there, and the prospect of being on my own so far away unnerved me. I needed the comfort of a few names I could call in an emergency . . . . [So] I wrote everyone I knew, asking, 'Do you know anyone in India?'

Her efforts produced a file of 18 names and addresses, primarily generated by 'weak ties' among her social networks: her dentist, a German friend, her aunt in Texas, and a New York cab driver all provided names of contacts in India.

Ms Andrus wrote a letter to each of the people whose names were provided, explaining that she was a writer, was planning to visit India, and would like to meet and invite them to dinner; she would call when she arrived. As she then describes in her travel article, 'The results were astounding' (*ibid.*: 8T). In India, an editor recommended by another writer became a close friend, opening her house as a 'home away from home' where Ms Andrus would stay between day trips. Other new friends became partners for music and art excursions, provided personal tours, and invited Ms Andrus to family events, including weddings. As she recounts in the travel article, 'I never dreamed that a few letters could help me make so many friends' (*ibid.*: 9T).

Tourism, of course, is one of the most visible forums of leisure experience in which people come into contact with others who are strangers. But the importance of social relationships should not be limited only to those potentially rare events of international travel. Tourism magnifies and makes visible the social networks that continually surround people. This story highlights the importance of patterned social relationships for leisure behavior and for the creation of social meanings that accompany the institutionalization of leisure.

The Social Networks of Leisure

Network analysis was introduced to the study of leisure, recreation, and tourism behavior over a decade ago. The introduction of structural analysis using network analytic techniques was proposed by Stokowski (1990a) and Stokowski and Lee (1991) as a rebuttal to, and extension of, dominant models of leisure that saw leisure as an outcome of interactions in small, primary groups. The social groups model proposed that people visited leisure places as members of family groups and friendship groups, but the model ignored contextual questions about how such groups arose from among people's already existing relationships of community. The intent of structural theorizing was to reorient research efforts to consider how social ties within communities fostered the grouping behaviors typically seen at leisure, recreation, and tourism places. Table 6.1 contrasts the perspective of the social groups model with that of the social networks approach.

While some sociologists and anthropologists had incorporated recreation behavior variables as part of larger network analyses (e.g. Bott, 1955; Fischer, 1982b), only a few leisure researchers have adopted structural theories or network methods in their work. There is currently only a small body of published literature about social networks in leisure, recreation, and tourism contexts, and there remains much potential for future development of structural theorizing and the extension of networks methods (Stokowski, 1992).

There are two defining characteristics of the small literature about leisure networks. First, researchers have primarily centered their attention on the reciprocal relational ties of affiliation, liking, and sentiment among kin and friends. This is in contrast to analyzing other types of relational contents, such

Table 6.1 Comparisons: social groups and social networks research in leisure

	Social groups research	*Social networks research*
Theoretical focus	Close social relationships and interactions in groups	Social relationships and extended community network structures
Context	Onsite recreation with family and/or friends	Community social networks in daily life
General approach	Within-group analysis of recreation participants	Analysis of differential activation of specific social ties across community networks
Analytic concerns	Social group influences on individuals (norms, socialization, rules) and individual psychologies (motivations, satisfaction of personal needs)	Interactional aspects of social relations; structural aspects of social networks
Meaning of leisure	Leisure achieved through group participation in recreation activities	Leisure achieved through relational ties and structural opportunities in all life contexts

as exchange relations, casual or transitory relations, or power relations, as they may be influential for leisure behavior. The locus of relationships of affiliation and sentiment is in human communities, so the community (studied as locale, and also as extended ties of belongingness) has become the primary setting for research about network ties for leisure researchers.

Second, researchers have generally focused on the leisure networks of individuals (egocentric networks), rather than on networks of corporate actors such as organizations or agencies providing recreation and tourism services. Both choices probably reflect the traditional philosophy among scholars to think of leisure behavior as individual, pleasurable activity accomplished during free time (Stokowski and Lee, 1991). In this chapter, a review of literature about leisure and personal networks is presented; later, the potential for research about organizational and interorganizational networks related to leisure is examined.

Despite the limited nature of early applications of networks research in leisure, structural analysis using a network model shows promise for advancing understanding of the social behaviors and meanings arising from leisure relationships. The networks perspective considers how the living environments of everyday community life stimulate leisure, recreation, and tourist behavior, and compels researchers to inquire whether free-time activity participation, in return, affects the broader relational structures of community life. Such theorizing ultimately raises questions about significant structural issues that affect leisure behavior. Questions about how leisure opportunities are distributed across social positions and roles, how social actors use power and position to obtain desired goals, and how different kinds of relationships produce differential access to resources and information can be addressed through structural analyses, and are critical for understanding the social significance of leisure phenomena.

In the discussion that follows, the small body of research literature about leisure, recreation, and tourism networks is reviewed and analyzed. Using the framework proposed by Stokowski (1990a), this review focuses on three general topics: structural antecedents, activities, and consequences of leisure behavior. First, the already existing structures of community relationships may be seen to foster leisure, recreation, and tourism participation. Second, new structural perspectives about the arrangement of visitors at leisure and recreation sites or tourist destinations may be uncovered. Third, structural researchers may find in network approaches the means to analyze the community and societal effects of leisure choices and behaviors. While the first two issues have been addressed by leisure researchers, the third topic has, as yet, unfortunately received no attention.

Influences of Community Networks on Leisure

Before they appear at leisure and recreation places or tourism destinations, people have already existing networks of community relationships with immediate and extended family, friends, neighbors, colleagues, workmates, and others. How do existing community interactions and ties influence personal choices for leisure experiences? To what extent do existing relational ties located in different sections of networks provide information, tangible resources, support, or companionship for behavior choices? Are there consistent network patterns that underlie particular types of leisure behaviors? Some of these questions have been addressed in the literature.

The travel-planning activities of tourists were analyzed by Eckstein (1983) using a networks approach. She found that destination information in two Michigan communities was usually obtained by tourists using informal ties and interaction with family and friends, who were perceived to be credible information sources, rather than through formal communication channels such as auto clubs, chambers of commerce, or other agencies. These conclusions confirm other non-networks research about the information-seeking behaviors of tourists (Gitelson and Crompton, 1983). Moreover, when Eckstein surveyed business managers in the two communities, she found that they had inaccurate perceptions about which information sources were most useful to visitors.

The use of family and friends as primary information sources was confirmed in research about the relative strength of ties within networks and between subgroups in a network. Stokowski (1990b) found differences between 'strong' and 'weak' relational ties in the information networks of elderly winter tourists to Texas. Strong social network ties (defined as close, friendly ties between people who knew one another well) were used by visitors to gather information about potential recreation and travel destinations. On the other hand, weak social network ties (defined as distant or casual ties between people who knew one another only slightly) provided access to the more general, day-to-day information needs of the travelers, such as finding health care or other service providers, or obtaining information about area activities. Moreover, this researcher found that clusters of strongly connected couples developed over time in the Texas trailer park, and that the members of these clusters returned to the same trailer park year after year in a type of a 'movable' community leisure experience.

The influence of community network ties on recreation choices was also studied by Stokowski and Lee (1991). In an analysis of community networks in a rural, timber-dependent town, the researchers found visible overlap between community networks of sociability and networks of recreation participation, though the network locations of significant others differed for men and women. Women reported that both their recreation and community socializing activities were undertaken primarily with other family members. Men, on the other hand, participated in recreation primarily with members of their own extended family or with friends. The effects of gender differences in community network structures on recreation and tourism participation decisions provides an interesting area for future research. This study is discussed in greater detail later in this chapter.

One example of research that extends structural theorizing beyond individual choice to analysis of community institutions in tourism planning is Cobb's (1988) research about the involvement of business leaders in local tourism development processes. She found that business leaders perceived to be more central in a community's social structure were more powerful in influencing decisions about community tourism planning than noncentral business managers. Influential business leaders in a community had extensive communication networks, and received more customer referrals than other business people. However, centrality was not simply a personal characteristic but a structural consequence. Centrality can be increased by 'being involved in community and professional organizations . . . [and] by talking to staff of tourism-related organizations both inside and outside the community' (pp. 166–7). This result is supported by other findings in the sociology literature about the importance of network centrality for collective behavior.

Social Networks at Leisure Places

The structure of network ties during onsite experiences at recreation places and tourism destinations has received only limited attention from researchers. Although much related work appears in the social groups literature of recreation research, and in studies of tourist types and travel group characteristics, there are few studies that specifically evaluate the network influences and consequences of specific relational patterns observed at recreation or tourist destinations. Do people who hold different positions in networks also take different kinds of trips or have different experiences onsite? Do particular kinds of network relational patterns encourage specific interaction opportunities between visitors and local people? What conditions allow network ties formed at recreation settings to persist even after events conclude?

Only a few studies about recreation networks address any of these issues. Allen (1980) analyzed the kinship and friendship ties among children attending environmental education programs at nature camps and found, not surprisingly, that when children were asked to choose partners for hikes, they most frequently chose others they knew. The implication is that when people are among others they do not know, recreation activities are used to reinforce existing kinship and friendship ties. These findings are a reminder to recreation managers that not all visitors are new to one another at recreation sites, and that pre-existing community social ties carry over into, and exert influence upon, the structure of new experiences.

On the other hand, the more relaxed, informal settings of leisure experiences, such as those seen at recreation and tourism places, may facilitate the development of new network ties. Levy (1989) analyzed the sociometric relations of boaters in a New Jersey marina, and diagramed the resulting sociometric patterns. She noted that boat owners with slips in two adjacent docks of the marina created an informally organized 'community' of affiliation. Subgroups of boaters showed 'intimacy and solidarity among themselves [and] lines of communication and interaction radiate[d] beyond cliques to construct an interwoven fabric encompassing the whole social system' (p. 320). This research suggests that shared interests and activities at recreation sites may provide opportunities for developing alternative social communities that both supplement and extend primary social ties in home locales.

An Illustration: Personal Networks in a Rural Community

Given the limited applications of networks structural theorizing in leisure research, and the wide range of methods in network analysis, it is not always evident how this research might be conducted. In the following pages, a brief summary of one study of personal networks is presented. This illustration describes the development of a single, very basic study of egocentric social networks in a rural Washington State locale, discusses data collection and analysis methods used, and outlines and critiques the findings. A more complete discussion of the methodology and results of this study can be found in either Stokowski (1988) or Stokowski and Lee (1991).

The Eatonville study

The purpose of this exploratory study was to analyze the effects of community social network ties on individual leisure choices and recreation participation behavior. Findings from sociological and anthropological networks research have suggested that people maintain repetitive and potentially predictable patterns of community interaction and social involvement (Bott, 1971; Wellman, 1979; Fischer, 1982b). Extended to leisure, networks thinking implied that leisure could be conceived not only as group-based performances of activities but also as the outcomes of existing social relationships that arose in community life. Therefore it should be possible to predict from the types of community network ties surrounding a person to his or her potentially repetitive and predictable leisure behaviors.

The study was a small part of a larger research project focusing on dispersed recreation use of public forest lands. The research was conducted in Eatonville, a rural timber-dependent community in western Washington State. In 1981, at the time of the study, the town had a population of about 1,000. Given the exploratory nature of the study, the researchers were concerned primarily with generating hypotheses for future work, so research followed a grounded theory approach (Glaser and Strauss, 1967).

In addition, the researchers decided to focus on egocentric social network patterns rather than on the overall social network structures of the community. For purposes of the study, it was thought to be important to understand how subjects were linked in interpersonal relationships to other people, regardless of whether the others lived within or outside the locale. The types of relational patterns among people were important, not the distribution of all relations across the geographic locale of the town. Bender's (1978: 7) idea that 'Community . . . is best defined as a network of social relations marked by mutuality and emotional bonds' was an appropriate theoretical basis for the research.

A sample of 25 households was chosen using a systematic sampling method with a random start. Selected households were visited by a researcher and both male and female heads-of-household were interviewed. In all, 44 interviews were completed, including 24 with females, five of whom were single heads-of-households, and 20 with males, one of whom was a single head-of-household. The interviews could be described as 'guided conversations' in which the researcher came prepared with a set of topics, around which questions were asked of respondents. This is an appropriate technique for exploratory research with an incompletely defined theoretical model.

During the interviews, respondents were asked to talk about the extent of their participation in outdoor recreation activities, and were also asked to describe their weekly leisure pursuits (defined as pleasurable individual or social activities). Participation frequency, seasonal variations, use of specific resource areas, and recreation partners were recorded. Respondents were also asked to describe existing interpersonal relationships with immediate or extended family, friends, neighbors, workmates, colleagues, and others in local organizations, and to comment on specific qualities of those relationships (content, frequency, and duration were recorded; other interactional network criteria, such as reciprocity, could not be determined from this research).

Based on answers to questions probing the relationships between subjects and their named others, egocentric social network patterns were drawn for each individual, and two measures were created. First, each social tie was rated on the expressed strength, or closeness, of the relationship (interactional network criteria). This rating was based on the frequency of communication, extent of shared interests, and general distance between residences. Then an aggregate strength measure (a proxy measure of network structure) was created by summing the strengths of all relationships within the categories of immediate family, extended family, and friends. The concept of strength of ties was operationalized only to a gross level (strong, medium, weak) owing to the nature of the conversational data.

Relationships classified as 'strong' were those in which the subject and others had frequent contact, shared interests and activities, communicated often, or exchanged information or goods. Conversely, a relationship classified as 'weakly tied' was one where the subject and others saw each other infrequently, lived some distance from one another, and considered each other to be only casual acquaintances. A category for 'moderate-strength ties' was included to accommodate ties which had characteristics between the levels of strong and weak. It was possible for a subject to have no strong ties, or to have aggregated strong ties in more than one category of others.

The classification of strong, medium, or weak should not be viewed as a value placed on relationships (i.e., a strong relation is 'better than' a weak relation). The rating refers only to a relative ordering of a subject's social relationships with others, based on frequency, content, and involvement. As Granovetter (1973) has pointed out, social ties of various obligation serve very different, but equally important, functions.

Analyses of the data included comparisons for (1) individual differences in social relationships and leisure behaviors; (2) differences in network structural patterns and recreation behaviors; and (3) comparisons of independent and joint network patterns and recreation behaviors between husbands and wives. The network analyses were completed through visual comparisons and the reduction of egocentric network patterns into generalized types. Since the detailed findings are presented elsewhere, only the most important conclusions are outlined here.

Social relationships
Of 44 total respondents, over half (*n* = 26; 59 percent) reported that their strongest social ties were with spouses and children in their immediate families, while another 23 percent (*n* = 10) reported strongest ties to extended family members, and about 21 percent (*n* = 9) reported strongest ties to friends. Five individuals (about 11 percent) reported no strong ties at all, and several subjects reported no ties to specific groups of others.

When the social ties of male and female respondents were compared, more females than males (69 percent, compared to 31 percent) reported that the immediate family was the center of strongest social ties. This was true for both married women and women who were single heads-of-households. A larger proportion of males than females had strongest ties to extended families (60 percent of the males, compared to 40 percent of the females) and to friends (89 percent, compared with 11 percent). These results were found to be statistically significant at the $P = 0.05$ level.

These network data indicate that the social worlds of male and female respondents had very different forms. Most female subjects reported that their strongest social ties were to members of their immediate families (spouse and children), while many male subjects reported that their strongest social ties were primarily with members of their own extended families (especially their fathers). The divergent orientations of these networks reflect the social positions of women and men in this resource-dependent community, and indicate that men and women used sociable ties in different ways, depending on their structural circumstances.

For example, about 54 percent ($n = 13$) of the women were housewives and did not work outside the house; several other older women had also not worked, or had worked only part-time. Their social networks were shaped by the requirements of child care and bringing up a family. Among this sample, a woman's *leisure* was what happened in the round of daily socializing, meeting at the grocery store, talking on the phone, or visiting around town. Children, kin, neighbors, and friends intersected in various sociable ways that were not easily translated into a list of 'recreation activities.' Recreation activities were 'events' that occurred at defined times. Leisure, on the other hand, was part of life.

For men, recreation events were primarily activities of involvement with other members of their own extended family or friends. In this traditional resource-dependent community, men tended to be closely tied to their own fathers, because fathers could provide referrals for employment opportunities and job-seeking assistance in timber and construction companies. Jobs were distributed based on 'who knows whom,' and so it was important that sons maintained strong ties with fathers who had the same occupations. The meaning of the kin social relationship was multifaceted. Recreation activities served to solidify work-related relationships by moving them into a leisure context. Men's networks, with more ties to others outside the immediate family, thus provided a variety of interaction opportunities.

The extended family also contained the most important sets of others for individuals who were single heads-of-household. Among this sample of single parents, community network involvement and recreation participation were facilitated through connections with one's own parents and siblings. Singles benefited from having a range of kin to call upon for assistance and sociability, for exchange of services (such as child care), and for emotional support. They also benefited from having, through the kin relation, 'weak ties' to friends of kin.

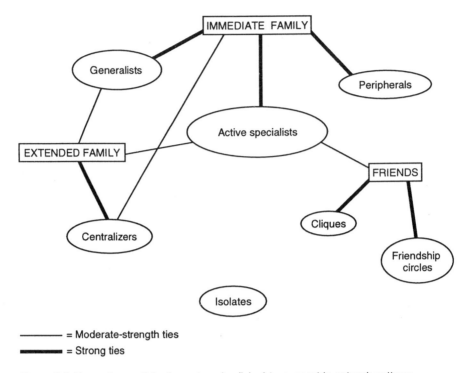

Figure 6.1 Recreation participation categories linked to egocentric network patterns

Structural patterns

Strong personal ties are only one segment of an individual's entire social network, and the choices made for leisure are likely to be influenced by the availability and strengths of a variety of ties with others distributed across the social network. However, the assertion that network ties are replicated in recreation behavior is confirmed in the Eatonville study. Among respondents reporting strongest social ties to members of their immediate families, 72 percent of all activities reported ($n = 19$) were also done with immediate family members. Another 14 percent were done with members of the extended family. Among respondents who reported strongest ties to extended family members, 56 percent of their activities ($n = 6$) were done in the company of extended family, 20 percent were done with friends, and 16 percent were done with immediate family members. Subjects reporting strongest ties to friends participated in 52 percent of their recreation activities ($n = 5$) with friends, 30 percent with immediate families, and 11 percent alone.

Qualitative and quantitative analyses of the interview data also resulted in a set of 'participation types' that illustrate how linkages across social networks potentially influence leisure behaviors. These types are diagramed in Figure 6.1. Some of the categories derive from traditional network analytic usage (e.g., isolates, cliques), while others were created to describe specific patterns in the Eatonville data. In this figure, only strong and moderately strong ties are diagramed.

Generalists, active specialists, and peripherals are people who have strongest social ties to members of their immediate families. These types differ from one another on the basis of the variety of relational ties they maintain with others across their social networks. In addition to their strong ties, peripherals had weak ties to extended family and friends, generalists had moderately strong ties to either extended family members or friends, and active specialists had moderately strong ties to both immediate family and friends. Overall, having more ties, and stronger ties, was beneficial for leisure. For example, active specialists participated in more recreation activities overall, and had so many potential social ties that they could choose specific partners for specific activities.

On the other hand, centralizers (having strongest ties to extended family and moderate strength ties to immediate family) had the benefit of cooperative ownership of recreation equipment, the shared 'family' knowledge of recreation opportunities (where to hunt, fish, or pick berries), and generally always-available sets of relatively close others for leisure. Cliques and friendship circles differed from all other network patterns mentioned in their reliance on strong ties with friends, with weak family ties with immediate or extended family members. Cliques were tightly knit, constrained groups. The primary clique identified in the Eatonville data was a group of 'town rowdies' who got most of their recreation excitement trying to stay one step ahead of the law. Their recreation activities included racing around town in fast cars, scouting out local forest lands for deer-hunting opportunities (including off-season poaching), and getting thrown out of local pool halls and bars. Friendship circles, on the other hand, were composed of neighbors and workmates who had similar interests. For example, a group of retired loggers met frequently at a local club for social purposes, such as lunches, card games, and sociable visiting.

Isolates were those people who reported no strong ties with others. These respondents were constrained by job schedules, or by having no local family and few local friends. They were socially uninvolved, spending leisure alone or in planned, irregular activities with workmates.

In summary, Figure 6.1 shows that among people who recreate primarily with immediate family members, there were several types of network relational patterns: generalists, active specialists, and peripherals, all differing in their ego-network structures. In addition, not all friendship structures were the same: among this sample, cliques and friendship circles were two distinct kinds of friendship relations. Finally, centralizers, active specialists, and generalists – people who recreated primarily with members of their extended families – had more network linkages overall, and more variety in their personal network structures.

Spousal networks

Two distinct network patterns were evident among the sample of 19 couples interviewed in the Eatonville study. First, seven couples exhibited patterns of reciprocal social ties, in which both spouses reported that their strongest social ties were to other immediate family members. Second, ten couples had patterns of nonreciprocal social ties, where one spouse (in this sample, always the female) reported strongest ties to immediate family, while the other spouse reported strongest ties to either extended family or friends. These two patterns were associated with varying degrees of community involvement and residential longevity. For example, couples with reciprocal social ties tended to have moved to Eatonville together, and had either structurally diverse networks (many different others in the network, including local and distant family and friends) or structurally limited networks (few other relational ties in the network; for example, one couple lived on the periphery of town, another had only recently moved to town).

For purposes of illustration, the contrasting network patterns of two study couples are presented in Figure 6.2. For couple A, reciprocal social ties between spouses are indicated with a double-arrow link; nonreciprocal social ties for couple B are illustrated as single-direction arrows from wife to husband and from husband to (in this case) friends. For the sake of simplicity, each spouse's relationships with children in the immediate family are assumed to be equal in strength, though in practice this may not always be the case. In both models, the large circle defines the members of the immediate family, and the square identifies the hypothetical boundaries of the locale, the community of Eatonville. Outside the square is the 'larger world' of meaningful social contacts who are separated by distance from the two couples under study.

Several structural differences are evident between the two couples. While there are many network features that cannot be determined from this representation (density of the networks, reciprocity of the ties, centrality across the entire community networks), it is clear that couple A maintains a larger-sized network than couple B. In A, the spouses report strongest ties to one another and their immediate families, and both also have ties to extended families and friends in the community and also external to it. Couple B, on the other hand, has a pattern of nonreciprocal social ties, and their range of linkages to others outside the immediate family is more limited. The wife reports weak to medium-strength ties with other members of her own extended family (but reports no ties to friends), while her husband reports that his strongest ties are with others in a group of male friends. At least some of the network differences between the two couples might be described in part by their relative longevity in the community: couple A moved to Eatonville together 11 years ago, but the husband in couple B was born in Eatonville and has lived his entire life there, while his wife moved to the community three years ago when they married.

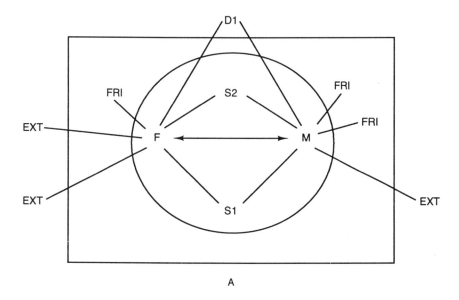

A

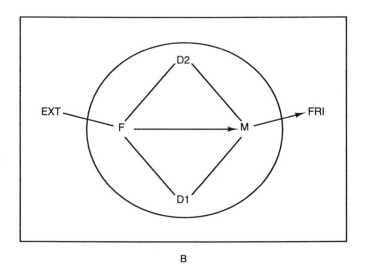

B

Figure 6.2 Reciprocal and nonreciprocal network patterns: two couples. A: reciprocal ties; B: non-reciprocal ties

The structural differences seem to be reproduced in recreation participation. Overall, couple A engaged in more total activities than the nonreciprocally tied couple B (an average of 11.5 to 5.5 activities), a trend that seems to be stable for at least the husbands in the Eatonville study. The wives generally averaged fewer total activities than their husbands, but the total remained constant whether females were in reciprocal or nonreciprocal relationships (suggesting that wives have other structural influences, such as the presence of young children at home, affecting their free-time choices). That couples in reciprocal relationships might participate in more activities overall than couples in nonreciprocal relationships raises several questions. Is this pattern common across society; that is, to what extent do all couples fit into the aggregated categories of reciprocal or nonreciprocal relationship patterns? How are new activities initiated within each pattern, and how do the relational patterns change over time? What do these patterns mean for personal and familial well-being, and for the experience of leisure in life?

The Eatonville study is admittedly preliminary and exploratory; data reflect the relational and behavior patterns of only a small sample of people. And, given the small number of couples ($n = 19$) interviewed, it is unwise to make generalizations about the influence of conjugal networks for leisure. Though limited, these data do raise questions about how the social network patterns of spouses influence leisure behaviors of families. While no preconceived value should be placed on the benefits of either reciprocal or nonreciprocal patterns of social ties, it would be interesting to know how each type contributes to overall life satisfaction and personal well-being, and to social isolation if a spouse is widowed or separated. Future research should investigate how the connectedness of the overall network surrounding each spouse in a couple may influence the activation of relationships for leisure.

Discussion

The Eatonville study suggests that social relationships and network structures may influence leisure in at least two ways. First, direct social ties between people provide opportunities for recreation behaviors to occur. Second, the 'collective influence' of social network ties surrounding individual actors may indirectly influence leisure by connecting people to sets of potentially significant others, such as friends of friends, who may have latent influence on leisure. The study of 'who will recreate with whom' becomes, under structural analysis, a function of an individual's position in a network of social relationships, and the further characteristics of extended linkages radiating out from others in that network.

That is, how people make decisions to choose activities, and how they group together onsite, may already be partly determined by their involvements in community relationships and networks which link them to specific categories of others. In addition, social ties activated for recreation follow through into community life after the recreation experience, and are likely to be reflected in other kinds of community involvement, such as work and other neighborly exchange relations.

Results from the Eatonville study indicate that leisure is not a 'residual' amount of time or a category of activity, as suggested in earlier research under traditional models, but a meaningful context of human experience. In leisure, recreation behaviors and meaningful realities are consequences of human intention and interactions across social networks. These relationships include not only dyadic involvements at onsite recreation places but also the extended community social networks which stretch across several different contexts of human experience.

Organizational Networks

As illustrated by the preceding discussion, networks research in leisure is currently characterized by a focus on the micro-level encounters of personal experiences and the strands of social ties extending outward from individual recreation or tourism activity participants. Researchers have yet to broaden their analyses to consider leisure networks on a large scale, such as ties within or between organizations or other complex collectives. However, leisure involvement is not only the product of individual choice and free will but is also structured by the range of opportunities made available by the production system that contains leisure services and places. Moreover, the relations between and among leisure service providers influence agency competitiveness, policy development, and resource management issues. One potential starting point for research about the influence of large-scale social collectives on leisure provision and experience is in the area of organizational and inter-organizational networks.

In sociology and anthropology, the study of organizational networks has achieved significant repute. In this research, attention is directed primarily to exchange relations, or relations of power and influence, as they structure market and political behaviors (see, for example, White's (1988) analysis of industrial markets, and Galaskiewicz's (1979) study of exchange relations between community organizational elites). In these and other organizational network studies, the general questions of interest are the same as those supporting research about egocentric social networks: how are the relations between organizations (or markets or nations) patterned, and what do the structural arrangements of those relations mean for the behavior of the entities under study?

While leisure researchers have not specifically studied organizational networks, there is evidence that such research may be on the horizon. Several recent journal articles, while not using a networks methodology, have raised issues and questions related to exchange relationships among leisure organizations. For example, Searle (1989) analyzed reciprocity and power in exchange relations between city recreation directors and their advisory boards in several

Canadian provinces. He found that 'there were few elements of reciprocity present in the relationship between the directors and board members' (p. 360), and suggests that future research should consider other elements of satisfaction in voluntary organization membership situations. Stokowski *et al.* (1992) raise related issues in analyzing the social contexts of success and satisfaction among rural recreation leaders.

Additionally, in a study of interorganizational relations between public (US Forest Service) and private (chambers of commerce and tourism associations) tourism managers in Arkansas, Selin and Beason (1991) also documented low levels of collaboration and cooperation. They suggest several strategies for increasing awareness and improving collaborative relations between agencies involved in the production and delivery of tourism services, such as initiating familiarity tours and forming institutionalized partnerships. Steene (1991), discussing a university program in Sweden, also addresses problems of inter-organizational noncooperation, and suggests approaches for improving relations between tourism organizations. He, too, finds low levels of interagency cooperation, noting that, during their research, 'it became evident that [tourism] agencies were suspicious about each other' (p. 666).

Finally, the relationships between tourism interest groups, and their collective influence on public policy, were addressed by Greenwood (1992). He comments that tourism industries and executives contribute to public policy in ways that 'range from the provision of expert information to policymakers to full involvement in the implementation of public functions via self-regulatory mechanisms' (p. 254). However, given that these agencies and firms have competitive interests and represent various production sectors of the economy, 'there is a limit to the degree to which [they speak with] a single political voice' (p. 255) or influence public policy. While this research was not devised as a study of interest-group networks, it is clear that the issues raised would provide substantive material for a network analysis of interorganizational relations in the tourism field.

Each of the examples discussed above raises interesting questions about structured relationships on a macro social level. There appears to be great potential for these, and related, issues to be addressed with a network analytic methodology. In fact, given the ability of network models to represent dimensions of and changes to power relations, resource transfers, and collaborative activity on the system level over time, it is likely that organizational networks research will be the next type of structural analysis to develop in leisure research. The conditions of intersection and reliance between and among natural resource agencies, recreation providers, and tourism and environmental interests have both theoretical and practical consequences for the provision and experience of leisure.

Summary

The study of both interest and sentiment relations in leisure, recreation, and tourism provides an extension and elaboration of traditional and interpretive theorizing that forms the foundation of the sociology of leisure. Both types of relationships can be studied on a variety of theoretical and empirical levels, ranging from egocentric social networks to whole-community network studies, and to studies of interorganizational influence and power. Structural research under a networks perspective raises many interesting questions about the reciprocal effects of leisure behaviors on social structures, and of structures on behavior. New applications of leisure analysis, and reinterpretations of past research findings, are stimulated by structural research.

For example, a network structural approach to leisure might provide a new sociological interpretation for the model of the outdoor recreation experience presented by Clawson and Knetsch (1966: 33–5). The authors proposed that the 'recreation experience' involved five phases: (1) anticipation, including planning; (2) travel to the recreation site; (3) the onsite experience; (4) return travel; and (5) recollection. Researchers have primarily analyzed the onsite, consumptive aspects of recreation suggested in this model, ignoring socio-lhgical aspects of both prior community linkages between people that stimulated recreation groupings, and potential future linkages that could result from recreation participation. In comparison, the structural model locates leisure in the broader networks of community, and attends to the anticipatory, onsite, and reminiscent phases of the recreation experience.

7

A critique of leisure
networks research

The principal issue with which I shall be concerned . . . is that of connecting
a notion of human action with structural explanation in social analysis. The
making of such a connection, I shall argue, demands the following: a theory of
the human agent, or of the subject; an account of the conditions and consequences of action; and an interpretation 'of structure' as somehow embroiled in
both those conditions and consequences.

(Giddens, 1979: 49)

Introduction

Efforts at a structural sociology of leisure are currently only in a preliminary
form, and there is much work to be done before a coherent body of knowledge
can be advanced. However, the research work discussed in the previous
chapter has merit in attempting to extend theoretical and methodological
approaches to leisure in order to accommodate issues of social context. These
studies provide a foundation for future exploration of structural theorizing
and analysis. In this chapter, the existing structural agenda of leisure research
is evaluated, and findings from the Eatonville study are used to generate
several hypotheses for further research. Two additional important issues are
then raised: the nature of 'meaning' under structural analysis, and the need
for facilitating micro–macro linkages in the analysis of behavior and structure.
Potential solutions to these problems, drawn from phenomenology in the first
case, and Giddens's theory of structuration in the second, are suggested.

The Influence of Social Networks on Leisure

How do social relationships and network structures influence leisure and
recreation? Drawing specifically from the findings of the Eatonville study,

several hypotheses can be advanced. First, in a general sense, network size is important for leisure participation, though the specific relation between numbers of others and leisure experience is currently unclear. Certainly, having many other relational ties (or at least 'enough' other ties) provides a social actor with information sources, material and helping resources, and sources of social support, any of which may translate into leisure opportunity. In Eatonville, having large extended family networks provided opportunities for greater leisure socializing and recreation activity for both men and women. Having smaller social networks, or networks composed of primarily non-significant ties, contributed to social isolation and fewer recreation activity involvements.

However, having many other linkages in one's own personal network may be less important than having some *specific* others related among themselves within networks. Greater proximity and increased density among social relationships across networks may provide wider opportunities for a variety of social behaviors, including leisure, to emerge. In Eatonville, when extended family members lived near a respondent, and when these others saw one another and the subject often, the result was an increase in opportunities for recreation. It may be hypothesized that dense networks and close, proximate social ties create a wide range of socializing opportunities for both the subject and his or her immediate family of spouse and children.

Highly dense networks create opportunities, but also have costs. These networks placed constraints on a social actor's free-time behaviors. For example, some extended families 'always' got together for Sunday brunch, and some fathers and sons 'always' planned an extended hunting or fishing trip together in the fall. The extended family and friends in these networks, like some of Bott's (1955) urban families, exercised varying degrees of social control and influence over the behavior of both the subject and his or her immediate family as well.

In addition, the more social ties one maintains, the more likely it is that 'weak ties' will develop. The Eatonville data suggest (in support of Granovetter, 1973) that weak links were activated more frequently for instrumental reasons in recreation, whereas strong social ties produced leisure sociability. For example, in Eatonville, weak ties were used to gain access to private forest lands for hunting, camping, and huckleberry and mushroom picking. These ties were also utilized for job-seeking among foresters and construction crews.

It may be hypothesized that the frequency of interpersonal interaction has importance for leisure (though not necessarily recreation activity involvements), but it is unclear whether this is a direct relationship. In Eatonville, the others a respondent talked to most frequently were the same others identified as partners in sociable leisure relationships. While more frequent communication may be an indicator of sociability in general, greater amounts of communication were not a requirement for shared recreation participation. It could be hypothesized that ties of leisure sociability overlap recreation ties under the following circumstances: when people have small networks, or dense networks, or networks containing multiplex ties. In the Eatonville data, leisure and recreation partners overlapped for some couples with reciprocal ties (when networks were small), and for persons having large numbers of extended family living locally (dense networks and multiplex ties).

The Eatonville study was designed to explore the relations between social structures and leisure behaviors. As such, it represents a useful preliminary research effort in applying structural theories and methods to leisure. The Eatonville study, along with the other research studies discussed in the previous chapter, also suffers limitations that prevent a full exploration of a structural sociology of leisure. Several of these problems are discussed below.

Given the preliminary character of structural research in leisure, there is great need for specification of theory and refinement of methods. Much of the current networks research in leisure focuses primarily on the characteristics of relationships and interactions rather than on analyses of networks structure. Future research efforts must refine measurements of interactional criteria, such as reciprocity and tie strength, and, more importantly, must devote greater effort to analyzing specific structural variables, including network size, density, and relational distance. This is especially important for expanding analyses beyond pattern identification and description among egocentric social networks.

Networks research in leisure currently involves primarily exploratory analyses of small samples of respondents. Given these conditions, it is difficult to obtain reliable data about relational reciprocity and network density. More effort needs to be made to consider the distribution of social ties across entire social communities in order that summary measures do not have to be contrived. For example, the measure of strength of social ties used in the Eatonville study was derived by summing distances between individual relationships within categories of others. It is unclear whether or how this procedure biases the outcome of network analyses; it certainly results in only a generalized approximation of network ties, rather than a direct accounting of relational linkages.

Future Leisure Networks Research

Structural research under a social networks perspective offers researchers the opportunity to reconceptualize critical contextual aspects of leisure, recreation, and tourism experiences. However, research efforts are currently only in the formative stages, and more work is needed in at least three broad areas: (1) analyzing how community-based social relationships foster involvement in activities and decision-making about leisure choices; (2) analyzing the importance of variations in the social structuring of visitors at leisure places for onsite coordination, between-group interaction, and future participation; and (3) considering how and in what form the social ties of leisure experiences might persist in other contexts of community and societal life in the future.

Structural theorizing proposes that the social behaviors of leisure are governed not only by immediate relational ties with close, significant kin and friends, but also by the collective influence of relational patterns across social networks. Leisure behaviors can be seen both as the product of variations in social structure and as a stimulus for specific structural arrangements that arise subsequent to leisure participation. For example, researchers might hypothesize that network density affects behaviors of individuals engaged in leisure as tourists: individuals with more highly connected networks may be likely to travel primarily in groups of family and friends and may require amenities that are group-oriented and traditional; tourists with less dense networks may be more independent and unconventional in their travel choices. Each network type probably requires unique kinds of information resources and destination services. Alternatively, when tourist behaviors are taken as independent variables, researchers might use network methods to test specific hypotheses about the effects of tourist interactions on regular patterns of host community communication.

Several issues remain problematic in the structural analysis of leisure networks. First, since many people visit leisure places in the company of others, the extended ego-networks of social relations that radiate out from each group member should be analyzed for regularities in network size, shape, and composition. Different kinds of groups -- families with children, group tour members, couples -- probably use different segments of their networks to obtain information and resources that enhance the leisure experience. Are certain network features typical across different types of primary groups? If so, researchers and leisure service providers may be better able to predict and understand how to reach nonparticipants, motivate those who feel constraint, target messages to audience members, and enhance social benefits through relational ties among and between visitor groups.

In future leisure research, it would be illuminating to include some psychological measures of personal happiness, life satisfaction, and individual and communal well-being. It would be particularly interesting to study whether and how leisure sentiments change over the life course as a result of changes in network structure and involvements. Matthews (1986), Moody (1986), and Larson and Bradney (1988) discuss the meaning and utility of family and friend networks for mitigating negative consequences of aging.

Second, all people have networks of social relationships, but not all networks have the same shapes and patterns. Network size varies, as does network composition, network density, the strength of ties (whether individual ties between nodes are strong, weak, or absent), and other interactional and structural features. These variations are important for whether people are happy, healthy, lonely, involved, or isolated, both in their leisure time activities or in their lives more generally. Researchers in gerontology and sociology have addressed some of these issues, but specific consequences for leisure behavior are uncertain. Do people engage in leisure in order to extend and diversify their networks? How do ties formed during activities influence later life? Answers to these questions might help leisure service providers structure social interaction opportunities in order to enhance social support and personal satisfaction.

A related issue concerns how well different social networks 'map over' one another. Leisure researchers have assumed that social relationships activated for leisure have features that distinguish them from work relationships, and, further, that leisure is only one element of friendship and kin interactions. These assumptions may be translated into a question that has empirical as well as theoretical importance: are different parts of *whole networks* activated for leisure, or are different parts of *specific relationships* activated? In other words, do people have one set of friends at work, and another set of friends with whom they recreate or socialize – or do they have one set of friends, some of whom they work with, and some of whom they choose to recreate with? This is theoretically important for understanding the patterning of leisure relationships across networks, and it is also of practical concern for people who might like to find new partners for recreation. How does one locate activity partners who might also be agreeable companions?

Third, social networks research in leisure, recreation, and tourism is currently characterized by a focus on close, affective relationships of community and sentiment within limited network structures. Exchange relations (those dependent on interest, such as market or power relations, regardless of personal sentiment) across broad social systems have been largely ignored, even though they are the subject of much of the mainstream sociological research about networks. The notion of exchange as a basis for leisure behavior is likely to be most relevant on the organizational or corporate level of analysis, though there may be cases where individuals interact with others on an exchange basis. For example, tourists may form exchange relationships with local people (perhaps in bartering for goods) or even other tourists (vacation house-swapping comes to mind as one example of this type of relationship). Structures of gift-giving behaviors within leisure networks may be another example of sociable exchanges that should receive more attention from leisure researchers.

One specific areas of tourism research that may be affected by a network structural perspective and a focus on exchange behavior is that of host–guest relations (Smith, 1989). This research topic should be broadly conceived to address not only the direct interactions between visiting tourists and community residents, but also the relations between local and external tourism promoters, relations between external resort or hotel operators and local laborers, relations between tourist-trading governments, relations between local and external environmental interests, and other relationships of significance in the production of tourist destinations. Williams and Shaw (1992: 139) comment that 'there has been a tendency to view the host community as homogeneous,' though only some community members are directly affected by tourism development, while others are indirectly affected. They continue,

> [There is a] need to reconsider the framework of much of our research about social relationships generated by tourism. Instead of focusing narrowly on these relationships in their immediate setting, we need to be aware of the broader economic and societal context. (p. 141)

The network structural approach can be useful in providing a reinterpretation and extension of the host–guest literature in tourism.

Networks researchers should look more closely at how various kinds of relational ties might create diverse consequences for individual and corporate behaviors in leisure contexts. The current focus on affective, sentiment relationships is reasonable, given previous findings about the significance of close personal ties among family and friendship groups in leisure. However, other types of relationships have yet to be considered in the analysis of leisure behavior. Not all that happens in leisure is likely to be positive, freely chosen, or rewarding.

In addition, not all relationships are created equal, and the concept of relational inequality might be of some importance in research about the relations between recreationists and leisure service managers or providers, or visitors and community residents. In fact, many case studies about cultural aspects of tourism describe disparity in social interactions. For example, researchers suggest that native life-styles are adversely affected by tourists, and that authentic experiences are contrived for the benefit of visitors. These findings suggest that structural theorizing about leisure relationships should consider the entire range of horizontal relations of affiliation and solidarity, as well as vertical relations of power, ownership, and authority.

Fourth, the study of how leisure behaviors influence future community interactions and involvements is largely ignored in the literature. Current structural research in leisure has focused primarily on studies of the influence of social network relationships on leisure, disregarding the influence of leisure on relationships and networks. Do relationships formed in leisure have lasting effects on the shapes and densities of individual or community networks? How are networks and network features transformed as a result of leisure participation? Social relationships that originate in or are enhanced by leisure behavior create possibilities for future interactions in broader community life. Whether these contextual affiliations or exchanges have significance and meaning for people in other community settings is as yet undocumented. Topics for future study might include how leisure promotes formation of new relationships beyond small group ties, what form new relationships take (do relationships begun in leisure contexts gain multiple contents over time?), and the consequences of leisure relationships for other spheres of community life.

Related to this issue are questions about the role of leisure relationships in facilitating transfers of social goods and services that are not inherently related to the leisure system. Certainly networks of leisure relationships influence the distribution of what may be called personal and social leisure benefits among people (Driver *et al.*, 1991; Mannell and Stynes, 1991). But leisure relationships may also serve to stabilize other kinds of social systems, such as communication systems, personal and social welfare systems, economic systems, and social knowledge systems. For example, Boulding (1989: 674) suggests that

> A loosely coupled structure . . . with a lot of informal relationships [such as] chit-chat on the golf course and that sort of thing, is less likely to have . . . corruption of information and, hence, is more likely to be adaptable and to survive.

This suggests that leisure may persist across society not only to provide a sense of personal freedom and pleasure but also because patterned relationships of leisure facilitate information and resource transfers across more generic social systems. Perhaps leisure is an integral social arena in all societies because it can provide a separate, unconstrained context for critical reflection and evaluation of the workings of other systems.

Finally, the application of structural approaches in leisure broadens understanding of leisure as a context of socially significant behaviors and meanings of communal life. Leisure systems contain a variety of social actors, from individuals to corporate entities, arranged in various levels of formal and informal organization, each having more or less extensive social environments. The case has already been made that relationships and networks have meaning for individuals and their personal behavior. Additionally, at least some of the network systems of leisure are international in scope, and their effective operation has major social and political implications. Structural theorizing and social networks research offer broad, encompassing perspectives from which to consider societal meanings and values of individual and corporate behaviors enacted in the context of leisure.

A Remaining Problem: Meaning

A significant drawback to a structural perspective in leisure is that the analytic process may be misinterpreted as deterministic, as simply another example of a machine-like system in which social structures define the boundaries and expressions of individual-level social actions. It has been the careful intent of this volume to suggest that current structural perspectives in sociology do not necessarily imply a fateful determinism, and that social network methods actually promote analyses of reciprocal relationships between individual action and social structure. That is, structure is seen as both a social creation produced from intentional (and sometimes unintentional) behaviors of humans, and also as an influence on micro-level activities.

However explicit this point may be, it is still difficult to account for the nature of meaning in individual and collective action. As used in this book, the term 'meanings' is defined broadly, and suggests both individual and social coherence about the nature of reality. Meanings are properties of both individual and collective social actors: persons may have meanings about their behaviors, and meanings may also be collective, held by sets of social actors.

In much of the research about leisure, meanings are assumed to be primarily individually based, and to take the form of psychological orientations, such as motivations, satisfactions, descriptions, or explanations of personal benefits received from leisure. These assumptions, centered as they are in the individual, separate the process of 'meaning-making' from broader social influences, relying instead on the abilities of individual actors to identify and label their own sentiments. A structural theoretical perspective, however, takes a vastly different approach to the nature of meaning.

Structural research about meanings begins with the assumption that meanings are social, the products of relational involvements. Meanings arise from the influence of interpersonal social ties, and also from the collective influence of extended social networks of ties of community among people. The processes by which meanings become adopted, and later institutionalized, by members of a society are social processes arising from engagement in interpersonal relationships. Meanings are cooperatively created and confirmed by people through social interaction. The patterning of social relationships in and across networks provides extended opportunities for validating and reproducing social meanings.

Analyzing the social structuring of meanings (and the network patterns of people who create meanings), though, differs from the actual identification of specific meanings and meaning contents. A structural perspective gives little insight about how a researcher might clarify particular meanings from all that transpires in any given social interaction. For this, a theoretical approach that focuses on the social construction of reality is more appropriate. Such a perspective is offered by phenomenology.

Phenomenology and meaning

Phenomenology originated within the philosophical debate over the human experience and knowledge of 'reality' (Stewart and Mickunas, 1974: 129). The German philosopher Husserl provided the initial statement of a theory of 'transcendental consciousness' where individual social action 'is conducted in a life world that is taken for granted and that is presumed to be experienced collectively as real' (Turner, 1982: 392). Alfred Schutz, an Austrian sociologist influenced by the work of G. H. Mead, grounded Husserl's philosophical approach in the interactionist theorizing of sociology. As Smith (1979) notes, Mead places man in a meaningful (intentional) world, and makes meanings social; that is, 'a man cannot generate a meaning on his own' (p. 13).

Schutz proposed that the world became meaningful as phenomena constituted in day-to-day living by individuals within the context of their social relationships (Wagner, 1970: 16). Knowledge and meaning are created through the intersubjective experience of human interaction, or, as Hamilton (1974: 135) explains, 'Our perceptions of reality are formed by the activity of social interaction, but not in some abstracted sense in which reality is external to the individual: interaction is the mechanism by which reality itself is *constructed* by social actors.'

There are several unique components of phenomenology that distinguish this perspective from more conventional sociological approaches. First is the emphasis on studying the common, everyday world of people. Berger and Luckmann (1966: 19) remark: 'Everyday life presents itself as a reality interpreted by [people] and subjectively meaningful to them as a coherent world.' It is in the world of everyday life that people become involved in the social relationships which provide them with knowledge and give meaning to their experiences. In day-to-day social interactions, people communicate to achieve consensus and understanding about what is real.

A second unique feature of phenomenological theorizing is its emphasis on regularly occurring social relationships. Schutz believed that 'living in the world of everyday life, in general, means living in an interactional involvement of many persons, being entangled in complex networks of social relationships' (Wagner, 1970: 30). The social relationships Schutz described are sustained in a 'communicative common environment' (Wagner, 1970: 31), where people use verbal and nonverbal strategies of communication in an attempt to reach consensus about their lived experiences. The term 'social network' implies that people have many concurrent relations of different kinds (from the immediate 'we-relations' to more distant 'observer relations') in which they participate as day-to-day occurrences. The phenomenological agenda, though, sees network analysis in a distinctly different light than the structural paradigm, holding that 'Any analysis of social structures must be in terms wholly dependent on interpretive criteria, involving understanding of the meanings which social relations have for those who engage in them' (Hamilton, 1974: 136).

A third unique feature of phenomenological theorizing is its emphasis on the intentional, social construction of realities. Social reality is not a naturally existing, objective occurrence, but a meaningful 'creation' or 'construction' arising from people's intersubjective relationships (Luckmann, 1978). The phenomenological agenda attempts to account for not only what individuals know but also what societies take as generally accepted, 'real' facts and knowledge (Berger and Luckmann, 1966). As Hamilton (1974: 136) points out, 'All knowledge is thus a construction produced in human interaction.'

Phenomenology approaches reality from the view of the interacting participants, and data-gathering methods that allow the researcher to 'see the world from the point of view of actors who participate in it [are required] . . . [the researcher] must spend time in the natural environment of those being studied' (Filstead, 1976: 65). Methods are principally ethnographic, qualitative, and naturalistic (Lofland and Lofland, 1984; Lincoln and Guba, 1985;

Agar, 1986), and include participant observation and in-depth interviewing in natural settings. Data analysis is often performed using a grounded theory, 'constant comparative' approach (Glaser and Strauss, 1967) allowing conceptual and substantive issues to emerge during analysis.

Phenomenology differs from other traditions of sociological theorizing in several ways. Most evident is that it takes as problematic what earlier sociologies took as 'given' – that is, the external, independent reality of social order that can be discovered, observed, and measured scientifically. Under phenomenology, an independent order exists only in so far as people 'create' reality and act upon their construction as if it were real. This kind of theorizing places no constraints on the social arrangements that may produce reality constructions: many kinds of relationships may contribute partial sensibility in developing intersubjective consensus about reality.

However, there are drawbacks to phenomenological sociology. Methods for scientific study and analysis of reality-constructing activities are not fully developed. There are few standardized practices for gathering data about how reality is constructed in the minds of individuals. Some scientists even question whether phenomenology can be a 'science' at all, since science is presumed to deal with objective empirical phenomena. And, when social life is continually being constructed and reconstructed, it is reasonable to wonder if there is ever a consistent, apprehensible object that can be studied scientifically. Smith (1979: 112) answers these criticisms by suggesting that

> Categories of the mind . . . are built into . . . sociology . . . but cannot in and of themselves account for any meaning system. Concrete meaning systems are generated by specific patterns of social contact and must be treated as the empirical items they are.

Phenomenology and the study of leisure meanings

In this volume, a phenomenological perspective is proposed as a link between the network structural analysis of patterned relationships and the analysis of the social construction of meanings through interaction. The phenomenological program suggested here emphasizes analysis of the structural distribution of social meanings, not studies of inner consciousness. In general, phenomenologists have not specifically attempted to map patterns of social meanings across sets of social actors (i.e., the structural analysis of networks of reality-constructing persons). Rather, they have been concerned with analyzing structures of social meanings, not structures of the egos and others who create these meanings. The mapping of socially created texts over the structure of social relations, however, may be one method for identifying and understanding the meanings of social experiences such as leisure behavior.

The merging of phenomenology with structuralism is not common in sociology, though several authors have postulated a connection between phenomenology and dyadic and extended social structures (McCall *et al.*,

1970; Macksey and Donato, 1972; Warnick, 1979; Wuthnow *et al.*, 1984). The fact that relationships of significance are often repetitive and patterned suggests that people act as if these relationships were real. Thus, both the reproduction of relationships and the creation of social meanings through mutual involvement and interaction in relationships are appropriate topics for study under both phenomenological and structural paradigms.

There are many interesting issues raised in blending these two approaches, and some have importance for leisure. One study that included an attempt to merge structural and phenomenological approaches was the Eatonville study, discussed in the previous chapter. In that research, the derivation of leisure meanings was accomplished using content analyses of the qualitative interview data, resulting in approximations of social meanings (meanings were not verified directly by respondents – a limitation of the study). The researchers looked specifically for meanings that not only were 'individual' interpretations of leisure, but also seemed to be interpretations held by a range of people (broadly conceived as 'social' interpretations).

For instance, many respondents talked about leisure as 'my free time to do what I wish,' describing how leisure was conceived as a specific 'time out' to recuperate and relax after required obligations were met. For these people, leisure involvement was time-constrained and had to be planned and regularized. For others, leisure was described as more of a central life interest, and respondents talked hopefully of a time when leisure might be enjoyed as a life-style, around which other responsibilities could be subsumed. Leisure was conceived as being a series of spontaneous, unconstrained life events. Researchers might hypothesize that these two general types of social meanings would be exhibited as different 'styles' of leisure, and emerge from within different network structures of interacting social actors. While the Eatonville study did not have a sample of sufficient size to test for differences in social network patterning, it may be proposed that different leisure meanings might be produced from egocentric network structures having differing compositions, shapes, densities, and other structural features.

The Eatonville data do provide some elaboration of the social meanings created and made real in the leisure experiences of subjects. For most male subjects, leisure meant a time to do recreation activities with extended family or friends. Leisure was equivalent to recreation activity participation. It occurred outside of work, but, like work, it took on qualities of instrumental purpose. One hunted for the thrill, but also to catch deer for meals; one camped with immediate and extended family, but the bigger agenda was fishing or looking for game; one maintained membership in a clique for the excitement, but also because of boredom.

For most housewives in the Eatonville sample, leisure was a context of sociability, a pleasant interlude away from children, chores, or required daily activities. Recreation, on the other hand, was an 'event' that required planning and coordination. It did not bring more personal time, but less. That is not to say that recreation was unenjoyable: recreation activities done with children were an escape from chores and were fun. But, as several women commented, being a housewife and mother was not leisure.

On the other hand, several retired persons in sample said there was no distinction for them between leisure and the daily happenings of life. As one commented, with retirement 'all the time is leisure.' Recreation events were generally identified as the time when their children and grandchildren visited (no matter what activities were done), or when couples got together with other couples for an evening of cards. For some of the retired men, recreation meant keeping in touch with former workmates by daily radio communications and by visiting the local clubs at lunch or after dinner.

No respondent had what could be called a 'leisure life-style' and the meanings of leisure among this sample were conventional. Leisure was not a way of life, but a small part of it. This conclusion suggests that the meaning of leisure as life-style is constructed in certain kinds of network structures and not others. For example, the pursuit of a leisure life-style probably requires that a person has a nonlocal, cosmopolitan orientation, a flexible job, and an independence from locale and family commitments. Relationships that allow the development of this spirit probably are arranged in complex social network patterns, containing diverse and extensive sets of relationships with many different kinds of others, in which the actor is located in either very central, or very isolated, positions.

The Eatonville study points out the need for micro-level interpretive work about the nature of social meanings to be conducted within the context of structural analyses. If the creation of leisure meaning depends on interaction between and among people who are arranged in patterned social relationships, it would be desirable to know the specific social processes responsible for the success of social actors in creating meaningful behaviors.

The network structural approach to leisure claims that social realities are cooperatively created by persons involved in meaningful interpersonal relationships. The key issue is how individual leisure meanings become 'social.' Social meanings are collective interpretations about the nature and experience of leisure that are taken for granted and assumed to be real. How well social meanings become institutionalized likely depends on the stability of leisure relationships across the entire range of complex relational environments of society.

Discussion

The utility of the phenomenological perspective is in its attention to the social constructions of reality accomplished by people in social relationships. However, phenomenology remains an incomplete statement of a sociology of relationships and meanings because it fails to specify exactly how social meanings are 'created,' and how people, once they enter into social relationships, construct and reconstruct reality. Phenomenology does, however, provide an intellectual bridge between theories of personal action and social structure. People stand in structural relation to many others in the world, and it is through interpersonal relationships that meanings about social reality are created. Leisure provides one social context within which this process can occur.

By postulating the 'socialness' of reality constructions, phenomenology creates the intellectual climate for considering exactly how realities are created within social relationships. It is the precise translation of philosophical phenomenological ideas into a scientific sociology which now requires scholarly attention, both in leisure research and, more generally, in the discipline of sociology.

Critique, and an Alternative: Giddens's Theory of Structuration

Phenomenology is a radical departure from mainstream social science, and there are widely-varying interpretations of the paradigm and its usefulness for sociological research. Few sociologists would accept whole-heartedly the hopeful combination of network structural analysis and phenomenology suggested above. Critics would claim that the two perspectives are incompatible in theory, that their methodologies cannot be juxtaposed, and that, in the final analysis, the combined approach still fails to coordinate macro- and micro-levels of analysis.

Further, the central problems of how to grasp social meanings and how to link individual behavior with structures and meanings across society remain only partly resolved in a phenomenological approach. Meaning is related to the intentionality of actors and, in Husserl's philosophical phenomenology, 'all consciousness is "intentional", in the sense that consciousness always has an object that constitutes it . . . intentionality is an internal relation of subject and object' (Giddens, 1976: 26). In cases where the object is another person, it is the internal constitution by an ego that creates consciousness of the other. The problem is that a philosophical intentionality results in a subjective, not a social, sociology. Giddens (*ibid.*: 17) notes that 'Schutz's philosophy remained wedded to the standpoint of the ego, and hence to the notion that we can never achieve more than a fragmentary and imperfect knowledge of the other.'

It is not only the other who cannot be reconstituted; it is the whole arena of social reality. Maines (1977: 239), reporting the critique of another sociologist, says that 'after examining Schutz's views on self–other interaction, [Perinbanayagam] concludes that phenomenology is "nothing more than a descriptive psychology of consciousness".' Giddens (1976: 36) acknowledges 'the primacy of subjective experience,' but adds, 'Having adopted the starting-point of a phenomenological reduction, Schutz is unable to reconstitute social reality as an object-world . . . the social realm cannot be constituted, in the transcendental sense of that term, from the intentional consciousness.'

So the phenomenological paradigm, as it currently exists, is an incomplete theoretical formulation of a sociology of knowledge and being. While attempting to account for the social realities and meanings created in everyday experience through social interaction, phenomenology begins with an ego and focuses on how the ego makes social constructions in the presence of an other. As a result, the other (and, in fact, all others in the world) remains incompletely defined. It is clear that an other must be involved for interaction to occur, but the mechanisms of involvement remain undeveloped. As a result, the specific linkages between individual psychologies and broader social structures remain unspecified.

The mutual dependency of action and structure

The blending of structuralism with phenomenology produces one potential, though problematic, solution to the problem of social order. An alternative solution is presented by Anthony Giddens, a respected sociologist identified most closely with the University of Cambridge. In a series of books written over the past two decades, Giddens critiques traditional theoretical approaches in sociology (functionalism, structuralism, and 'interpretative' sociologies – including hermeneutic philosophy and critical theory, ordinary language philosophy and ethnomethodology, and phenomenology), and develops a 'theory of structuration' that attempts to resolve deficiencies in previous approaches (Giddens, 1976, 1979). Subsequently, Giddens considers the methodological and practical consequences of the theory of structuration for various aspects of social life, including stability and change across social institutions (Giddens, 1979, 1984), notions of conflict and power in social systems (Giddens, 1984), and the understanding of modernity (Giddens, 1990).

In his review of social theory, Giddens concludes that sociology suffers from two interrelated problems: the lack of a coherent 'theory of action' that can account for continuous human behavior, and the lack of a theory describing how human action (what he calls 'agency') is intimately connected with the structuring of social systems across time and space. Giddens (1976: 15) notes that interpretative sociologies fail to comprehend that *'The production of society* is a skilled performance, sustained and "made to happen" by human beings' (emphasis in original) who rely on language skills and generalized social knowledge in an effort to effect desired outcomes. Likewise, structural sociologies elevate the importance of social systems but fail to retain an understanding of the integrated behaviors of social actors who create and populate those systems. Further, both types of social theory fail to account for time.space relations in social order, political and social change, or evolutionary processes in the analysis of society.

Thus Giddens proposes that the reformulation of sociological theorizing must begin from the premise that human agency is intimately bound to the structuring processes of social systems and, further, that all structuring processes must be conceived against a backdrop of time (history) and space (context). Giddens's structuration theory incorporates each of these elements, acknowledging that 'The key to understanding social order . . . is not the "internalization of values" [by individuals], but the shifting relations between the production and *reproduction* of social life by its constituent actors' (emphasis in original) (Giddens, 1976: 102). That is, social actors purposefully engage in continually negotiated communication processes with other social actors, drawing upon their mutual knowledge of past social practices to create, produce, and reproduce social systems of meaning and relationship. Actors are not all-powerful, though, and not all intended outcomes occur as planned, despite the intentionality inherent in social practices. Giddens (*ibid.*: 157) comments that 'The production of society is brought about by the active constituting skills of its members, but draws upon resources, and depends upon conditions, of which they are unaware or which they perceive only dimly.'

A central idea in the theory of structuration is that of the 'duality of structure.' Giddens (*ibid.*: 121, 127) says:

> By the *duality of structure* I mean that social structures are both constituted *by* human agency, and yet at the same time are the very *medium* of this constitution . . . structures only exist as the reproduced conduct of situated actors with definite intentions and interests. (emphasis in original)

All social actors, therefore, have some understanding (even if unarticulated, or unconscious) of the processes necessary to reproduce society, and it is their competent participation in society that ties human agency to the persistence of social systems. That is, social structures of 'rules and resources are drawn upon by actors in the production of interaction, but are thereby also reconstituted through such interaction' (Giddens, 1979: 71).

This application of the concept of 'structure' differs from more traditional uses in sociology. According to Giddens, structures should not be viewed as 'entities' that exist in the world (i.e., specific relationships among sets of social actors) but should be seen as the special properties of social systems. (Recall the citation in Chapter 4, when social structure was first discussed (Giddens, 1976: 121): 'A structure is not a "group", "collectivity" or "organization": these *have* structures.') Giddens would describe groups or other sets of people as 'systems' of regularized social action; he defines the concepts of structure, system, and structuration, as follows (Giddens, 1984: 25):

Structure(s):   Rules and resources, or sets of transformation relations, organized as properties of social systems.
System(s):   Reproduced relations between actors or collectivities, organized as regular social practices.
Structuration: Conditions governing the continuity or transmutation of structures, and therefore the reproduction of social systems.

Giddens's reformulation of social theorizing results in a new approach to the analysis of both individual action and social structural transformation.

Society can no longer be viewed as simply the aggregated sum of individual behaviors but must be seen as the simultaneous influence on and consequence of intended and unintended human agency. That is, 'The constitution of agents and structures are not two independently given sets of phenomena . . . the structural properties of social systems are both medium and outcome of the practices they recursively organize' (*ibid.*: 25). Human action is mediated by the structural properties of social systems, and social systems are reproduced through patterned social practices. Sociological methods which divide the two levels are inaccurate, according to Giddens (1984: 25), who comments,

> Analyzing the structuration of social systems means studying the modes in which such systems, grounded in the knowledgeable activities of situated actors who draw upon rules and resources in the diversity of action contexts, are produced and reproduced in interaction.

Giddens's critique of social theory produces new insights about some previously vexing, persistent sociological problems. For example, his insistence on the mutual dependency of agency and structure results in a social theory that bridges the gulf between micro and macro levels of social analysis so there is no wide separation between the behavior of actors and the behavior of social systems. As Giddens (1976: 22) emphasizes,

> the problem of the relation between the . . . [production and reproduction] of society by actors, and the constitution of those actors *by* the society of which they are members, has nothing to do with a differentiation between micro- and macro-sociology; it cuts across any such division.

Additionally, since time and space relations affect the performance and outcomes of social encounters, sociologists must attend to the ongoing experience of time and space in analyzing structuration processes. Giddens (1979: 202) remarks that these aspects are 'ordinarily treated more as "environments" in which social conduct is enacted . . . rather than as integral to its occurrence.' The time and space dimensions of social life, however, provide critical information that is needed for structuration processes. For example, social contexts place constraints on the size of collectivities that might gather, and also influence both who might be present or absent, and what kinds of interactions might be possible. Time influences the patterning of contacts such that, for example, ancestors feature in current memory even if there was never a direct personal relationship with the person 'remembering.'

Further, the theory of structuration provides an approach to the concept of 'meaning' in social action. According to Giddens (1976), meaning is not equivalent to motive, or intended outcome, and cannot be conceived as external to actors' social practices (that is, meanings are not independently 'contained' in social practices or social texts). Rather, 'Social life . . . is *produced* by its component actors precisely in terms of their active constitution and reconstitution of frames of meaning whereby they organize their experience' (emphasis in original) (*ibid.*: 79). The production of meaning should be seen as being continually negotiated between people so that 'the creation of frames of meaning occurs *as the mediation of practical activities*, and in terms of differentials of power which actors are able to bring to bear' (emphasis in original) (*ibid.*: 113). Thus, what is taken as meaningful is what social actors reproduce as meaningful in everyday routines conducted over time, but this is dependent on the relative social power among communicating actors. Giddens (1979: 83) notes that 'Power is expressed in the capabilities of actors to make certain "accounts count" and to enact or resist [normative] sanctioning processes; but these capabilities draw upon modes of domination structured into social systems.'

Finally, the theory of structuration proposes an explanation of institutional transformation across society by reducing the importance of social roles as 'given' positions (with associated predetermined norms) in social systems, and by 'treating institutions as chronically reproduced rules and resources' (Giddens, 1984: 375). Persistent, highly visible social institutions, such as religious practices, family forms, or leisure behaviors, represent coordinated patterns of human social practices, rules and resources that are entrenched, to varying degrees, within society. They illustrate the routinization of social practices and structures, and the taken-for-granted nature of much of social life. Economic institutions also demonstrate persistence. For example, Giddens (*ibid.*: 34) comments that

> The 'economic' cannot properly be defined, in a generic way at least, as concerning struggles for scarce resources. . . . Rather, the sphere of the 'economic' is given by the inherently constitutive role of allocative resources in the structuration of societal totalities.

In sum, the ordering of power and dependence relations through the reproduction of social interactions and practices results in the structuring of institutional systems, and the enduring repetition of such institutions in society.

Structuration theory and leisure research

While there are many interesting ideas embedded in Giddens's work, the usefulness of his approach for analyses of leisure phenomena has yet to be explored. A complete discussion of potential areas of intersection is beyond the scope of this volume; however, there are several notable features of his theorizing that may usefully extend the network structural analysis of leisure which is the central theme of this book.

First, the use of network analytic methods to analyze social structuration processes is not precluded by adopting Giddens's structuration theory. Haines (1988) describes the implicit convergence of network methods with structuration theory, concluding that 'Social network analysis would be improved by the introduction of the action component of structuration theory; structuration theory by the introduction of the system component of social network analysis' (p. 179). The strength of social network analysis in operationalizing relational concepts on all levels of social organization would provide further explanatory power for structuration theory. In addition to network methods, structuration theory, centered on the embeddedness of social meanings in language, presupposes some form of ethnographic analysis of social texts to uncover the structures of rules and resources that situate social meanings in time and place (Giddens, 1976, 1979).

Second, the structuration and transformation of institutions have implications for understanding the role of leisure in modern social life. For example, Giddens (1990: 12–13) proposes that 'Modernity . . . is *multidimensional on the level of institutions* . . . [and] the dynamism of modernity derives from the *separation of time and space* . . . the *disembedding* of social systems . . . and the *reflexive ordering and reordering* of social relations' (emphasis in original). These characteristics of modern social systems have implications for, among other things, the enactment of social relationships and the development of personal identity. In his analysis of the structuration processes of modernity, Giddens (*ibid.*: 119) concludes that 'The vast extension of abstract systems (including commodified markets) associated with modernity transforms the nature of friendship.' Friendship relations, formerly based in immediacy and in solidarity against the unknown world, now extend beyond the boundaries of locale or community. Moreover, a friend is not today defined primarily as a 'durable alliance' against strangers but as 'someone who protects the emotional well-being of the other' (*ibid.*). This critique raises questions about whether leisure presents one of the last social contexts of the modern world in which informal friendship relations and practices can be expressed.

Further, the creation of self-identity becomes more difficult in modernity, when institutionalized relations are in flux and 'an individual must find his or her identity amid the strategies and options provided by abstract systems' (*ibid.*: 124). Again, leisure contexts may provide a stabilizing influence on structuration processes related to interpersonal contact, meaning development, and the negotiation and confirmation of self-identity. Friendships, and leisure behaviors involving friends, are the expressions of structuration processes that reproduce the modern search for self-identity.

Under these conceptions of modernity, leisure (on the interpersonal, experiential level) may be hypothesized to contain the reciprocally produced and reproduced systems and structures of 'community' which provide meaning for the social practices surrounding friendship maintenance and personal identity development. Leisure, then, is sustained as an arena of social life in which people develop self-identities and find these identities confirmed by emotionally supportive friends in multiple, flexible contexts. Over time, leisure relationships reproduce the structures that foster friendly social ties, thus ensuring the permanence of leisure systems. (The flexibility and openness of communal relations of leisure, though, may trivialize both the enactment of leisure relationships and the development of self-identity as 'nonserious activity,' a risk that runs through modernity.) Correspondingly, on the organizational level, leisure might be conceived as the structuration of human behavior and meaning around leisure provision systems, including both common property resources (environmental 'goods,' such as parks or wilderness areas), as well as private recreational, environmental, and tourism resources.

Third, the theory of structuration returns leisure research to its earlier focus on 'context' as a significant issue in analyzing social interaction. The idea of 'leisure places' was developed and elaborated in interpretive leisure research primarily in reference to the social groups models of recreation behavior. In these approaches, leisure was conceived as an experience occurring onsite, at specific places, where recreation activities were conducted, generally in the company of family and/or friends. The problem with the social groups model is that it leaves social actors where it finds them: at recreation places. There is no attempt to understand how contextual aspects of leisure appear as the reproduced social practices and relations of actors who simultaneously are engaged in reconstituting society. As a result, the study of leisure – seen as simply the description of people at play – remains outside the main concerns of sociological research.

The solution to this problem may be found in directing renewed attention to the interdependence of structuration processes with the contextual nature of social interaction. Giddens finds this linkage most evident in the discipline of human geography, which, as he points out, 'has come to contain many of the same concepts, and to be involved with the same methodological debates, as sociology' (Giddens, 1984: 364). The immediate point of departure for leisure researchers might be found, as Giddens suggests, in a fuller understanding of how aspects of 'place' affect the reproduction of systems of social practices. That is, space is not 'empty,' waiting for action to occur: it is always 'social,' and intimately tied into the reproduction of social structures. Giddens (*ibid.*: 367) comments:

> The co-ordination of the daily paths of individuals within a given range of locales, plus what some researchers have called a 'sense of place', are concretized aspects of the duality of structure . . . the continuity of the biography of the individual is expressed in, and also expresses, the continuity of institutional reproduction.

Places are visible manifestations of the persistence of actions and structures.

Summary

This chapter began with a discussion of issues and hypotheses raised by an analysis of the social structuring of leisure behavior. Two significant issues that remain unresolved in a networks structural approach to leisure are: (1) questions about how meanings are socially created and distributed across social systems; and (2) issues related to the intersection of individual action and structural forms. Two alternatives for addressing these problems can be found in phenomenological research about social meanings, and in the theory of structuration presented by Giddens. Of these, structuration theory provides a more comprehensive perspective for addressing issues that are problematic in phenomenological and structural theories. Further, the theory of structuration is not incompatible with a networks methodology which analyzes particular social relations among specific sets of social actors. While Giddens's theory of structuration shows great promise, it is as yet undeveloped in leisure research. The use of any of these alternatives, however, is seen as a way to extend leisure research beyond traditional and interpretive theorizing.

8

Conclusions and consequences of a structural sociology of leisure

Einstein's space is no closer to reality than Van Gogh's sky. The glory of science is . . . in the act of creation itself. The scientist's discoveries impose his own order on chaos, as the composer or painter imposes his; an order that always refers to limited aspects of reality, and is based on the observer's frame of reference, which differs from period to period as a Rembrandt nude differs from a nude by Manet.

(Le Shan and Margenau, 1982: 3)

Introduction

For many years during the decade of the 1980s, a collection of figure skaters, both men and women, met on Sunday mornings at one of the ice rinks in Seattle. There, for two hours, the ice dancers skated, the nonskating spouses gossiped, and when the ice was being cleaned they all mingled around the coffee and pastry table. Ranging in age from about 25 to near 80, these skaters called themselves the 'Sunday morning skaters.' They were not an established 'group,' because participation varied by season and personal commitment. Nor could they be called a 'social world,' since these skaters were only one small part of the entire skating world of Seattle; these skaters and their significant others also had more complex and richer social relationships than might be observed among members of a single, activity-based social world. The most appropriate description of this collection of people is that they formed a locally connected cluster within the social network of the Pacific Northwest skating community.

The network relationships in which these skaters and spouses were enmeshed provided a variety of benefits, resources, and pressures. The cluster of people, family, and friends celebrated birthdays, anniversaries, and departures when people moved away. Some helped with sewing or beading skating costumes for others; some took photographs at skating performances and made pictures and tapes available for review; others loaned hats and mittens; small gifts were given on important occasions. The ties also extended beyond Sunday mornings. Lunches, dinners, and telephone calls were shared, several couples traveled together on vacation, and advice and emotional support were freely given when the need arose. In return, the network ties exerted good-humored 'pressure' on individuals to participate and to conform to expected behaviors. Potential boyfriends of a young woman were scrutinized, the communication styles of regulars were evaluated, absences from events were noted. But the loss of some privacy was a small price to pay for the warmth and caring among a very diverse, extended set of others.

Now, nearly eight years after the peak of the Sunday morning skating activities, time and distance have changed the social circumstances of many of the participants. Some people moved away, several stopped skating, others have died. Many of the relationships proved to be temporary, though the memories of past satisfying times remain. Some people who still live in Seattle continue to see one another, and letters are exchanged with those who were close but moved away. Sometimes, at a new ice arena in a new town, two skaters meet and find that they have friends in common as a result of ties with members of the Sunday morning skaters guild. The network cluster of years ago has disappeared, but the relationships endure.

This true story, reflecting the meaningful leisure of one small set of people, illustrates the social complexity of the leisure experience. Leisure is more than simply a series of special events separated from the reality of daily life. The people involved together in leisure often have multiple relationships beyond primary group membership. A structural approach suggests that leisure might best be conceived as a social context, part of daily life, reproduced in ongoing relationships among sets of people, and crossing boundaries and contexts of social life. In the following pages the conclusions and consequences of a structural perspective on leisure are discussed.

Reinterpreting Leisure

The focus on social structure assumes that social relationships are patterned and at least partially predictable, and that by studying the arrangements of order in social systems, researchers can begin to understand the behaviors of social actors as they coalesce within networks, and the influences of social structures on the actions and thinking of social actors. The network analytic approach to the study of structure provides a picture of social relationships that can be considered a 'geography' of ties in a social environment, where linkages among people have meaning for both action and structure. The analysis of leisure from a structural perspective stands in direct contrast to earlier approaches that see leisure as the outcome of choices made by

free-acting individuals who are constrained only by work and personal commitments or goals. In traditional approaches, psychological reductionism is
only partly mitigated by grounding leisure in daily life; leisure still remains
highly individualistic.

The lack of attention to the structural outcomes and influences of free-time
behavior produces a social psychology of leisure rather than a complete
sociology of leisure. Intersections between leisure and broader society remain
unacknowledged, their scope unknown. By ignoring context, researchers
tacitly and mistakenly assume that social structure is unchanging, and that
society, culture, and institutions remain static over time. A renewed awareness
of the importance of structure for leisure behavior is currently emerging
in calls by scientists for the study of 'context' in leisure (Kelly, 1992). For
example, Mannell and Stynes (1991: 470), reporting on a paper presented by
sociologist Erik Cohen at a conference on leisure benefits, remarked,

> For Cohen the major problem is the paucity of attempts to relate the benefits
> of leisure to the wider problem of developing a sociological or cultural perspec-
> tive on modern society, that is, how does leisure relate to the wider social struc-
> ture and culture.

The development of new interpretive approaches in research signals an
interest in relational aspects of leisure, and foreshadows a comprehensive
structural sociology of leisure. However, by remaining wedded to within-
groups analyses of leisure behavior, these efforts fall short of a structural
understanding. This book proposes a reinterpretation of leisure as a structured
social context containing social relationships, behaviors and meanings that
emerge from community interactions, and are patterned across extended
systems of structured social networks. The primary assertions of a structural
sociology of leisure are twofold: first, that social structure is produced through
communication processes and interaction in relationships enacted within
leisure; and, reciprocally, structural properties of social systems are reproduced through the patterning of relationships across networks, the social
construction of leisure meanings, and the enactment of recreation choices.

The basic assumption of structural theorizing using network analytic
methods is that characteristics of relational patterns, network systems, and
structuring processes are of greater importance in interpreting the behavior of
social actors than any personal characteristics or psychological dispositions of
the actors. This should not be translated as favoring structural determinism,
however. It is instead an explicit attempt to trace the patterned, relational
pathways between people that support leisure choices and meanings, and to
understand the consequences of specific kinds of patterns. As Giddens (1984:
169) notes, 'structure is always both enabling and constraining.' Moreover,
the analysis is not only in the direction of macro to micro influence: leisure
provides a context in which social actions and relationships are enacted,
reproduced, and institutionalized across society. These macro-structures (in

the traditional sense) reciprocally exert influence on the behavior of social actors by institutionalizing the appearance of stability, communal participation, and longevity.

The structural perspective presented in this book bears a closer resemblance to Giddens's (1979, 1984) theory of structuration than it does to other structuralist approaches that give primacy to structure over individual behavior. A sociological perspective that links micro- and macro-processes requires both a theory of action on the micro level, and a theory of structure that specifies the location and effects of those actions within broader social systems on the macro level. Giddens (1979: 69) calls this the 'duality of structure,' saying that 'the structural properties of social systems are both the medium and the outcome of the practices that constitute those systems.' Social structures are not objects that have an independent existence in reality, but instead are the intentional and unintentional constructions of humans, who are influenced to varying degrees by reliance on these very same structures. As Berger and Luckmann (1966: 60) comment, 'the objectivity of the institutional world, however massive it may appear to the individual, is a humanly produced, constructed objectivity.' They note that one of the aims of a sociology of knowledge is in understanding how people come to take the world they create 'for granted.'

Reinterpreting leisure under the perspective of structural sociology does not deny basic orientations of earlier leisure research efforts. Leisure remains important to people because, in practical terms, it is a social context characterized by free time, unscheduled activity, and relatively 'free' choice, away from work and other human responsibilities. In industrialized society, leisure is seen as desirable and pleasurable, bringing personal and social benefit. But the importance of interactions within the patterned social relationships of leisure cannot be underestimated. The structural perspective departs from other approaches by asserting that the behaviors and meanings of leisure result not only from individual conceptions of time, activity, and satisfaction but also from the influence of network relations and positions across society. Reciprocally, leisure is not a separate context of social life, but intimately connected to behaviors in other societal contexts.

The structural approach presented in this volume is not a single solution to analysis of leisure behavior. Leisure does not ·depend entirely on the qualities and characteristics of social relationships, but results from the influence of a variety of other conditions. For example, people take up hobbies, become mountain climbers, learn to play basketball, or plant gardens because they have certain kinds of interests and abilities. And people are born into different social, economic, and historical circumstances which affect their leisure opportunities. Leisure, like power and prestige, is not equally distributed across all people. But to the extent that personal experiences of leisure depend partly on social involvement, the networks structural approach can provide a means for theorizing about the patterns and meanings of social ties that support leisure behaviors.

A network structural sociology provokes questions about how specific kinds of social relationships structure personal behaviors, knowledge, and social meanings, and affect the reproduction of leisure across society. The relevant questions are those concerning both action and structure. Who are the others influencing behavior in leisure contexts? What are the characteristics of the social relationships and networks that surround people in leisure? What personal and social meanings are produced through relational interactions and the patterning of relations across networks? What are the consequences of relational contacts for the behavior of individuals, groups, and networks as a whole? How can people manage or manipulate contacts and ties in order to produce outcomes they desire? How do the social structures of leisure 'fit' within broader economic or political structures of society?

The structural perspective links micro and macro levels of analysis in social research. Individual behaviors of leisure are placed within broader social contexts, and leisure itself is seen as one theme in the concert of social life. The social significance of leisure is both in the individual experience of freedom and choice, and in how relationships and structures of leisure help mitigate human problems, foster cohesion in communities, alleviate personal suffering, maintain economic stability, and encourage political responsibility. These broader structural questions should be the very issues that frame sociological theorizing about leisure.

Unresolved Issues

There are many interesting issues raised by a focus on relational and structural aspects of leisure contexts. The most basic of these relates to how people and societies define 'free time' and identify appropriate behaviors within non-obligated time. How is leisure made central in life, and what are the processes by which leisure is institutionalized across societies? A structural perspective allows that the nature of work influences the definition of leisure, but seeks an explanation of the social processes that regulate the scope and availability of leisure opportunity on personal, group, organizational, and societal levels. Leisure is not a random occurrence but a structured system of people, settings, behaviors, and meanings arranged across time and space which contribute to social order in a variety of ways that can only be fully understood under a structural approach.

The structural perspective on leisure raises questions about whether leisure is 'freely chosen' or is at least partially determined by the structural criteria of relationships. Given that people live in social environments and are surrounded by many relational ties, personal choices are hypothesized to depend partly on the influence of others surrounding any given social actor. Relations and positions in social networks both constrain and facilitate an actor's behavior, but social structures may also be manipulated by the intentional activities of actors. There is a need for an overall theory of leisure specifying the reciprocal effects of structured relationships (both of interest and sentiment) on social actions and meaning.

While many actions are intentional, behavioral choices may also result in unintended outcomes that nonetheless influence future action. Social actors operate with limited knowledge, and often have little understanding of the patterns of relationships beyond their immediate experience. When actors attempt to 'order' their worlds, unintended consequences (such as relational overlap, or conflict in social ties) may occur across a network. Traditional leisure research is unable to deal with the unintended consequences of personal and collective choices, but a structural approach makes an effort to document outcomes beyond localized experiences by tracing paths of influence through relational ties and across networks. In this way, social effects related to the accumulation of knowledge across leisure networks, the elaboration of social meanings, the variable exercise of power or controls, or the distribution of resources can all be documented and evaluated across local and extended regions of networks.

However, the intended or unintended consequences of personal actions may not be limited only to leisure systems but may also extend beyond these to influence reciprocally other institutions. For example, to what extent do the social reproductions of leisure influence patterning of ties in other systems, such as work or political networks? The executive who golfs with a client broadens the contents of single relations, and creates at least marginally overlapping networks that provide potential openings for future interactions. Likewise, new friendships developed in leisure may either take the place of old friends, or may be incorporated into existing networks.

Alternatively, what kinds of constraints are exerted on leisure behavior by systems external to leisure? Political systems, such as governments and religious institutions, sometimes attempt to control or limit expressions of leisure; for example, by regulating holidays or manipulating activity choices (or by making rhetorical claims about certain forms of activity). Corporations market their products using subtle and overt leisure images and context. Can leisure practices subsequently influence corporate goals, directions, and policies?

Traditional approaches to leisure research tend to minimize the influence of others in the social environment on the development of individual motivations, satisfactions, or choices. However, it is likely that individual sentiments about leisure are real only to the extent that they can be socially negotiated and confirmed. Much of the social-psychological literature in leisure and recreation research could profit from the addition of contextual and structural variables discussed in this volume, since it seems nearly impossible to theorize about the complexities of individual behaviors and meanings without some understanding of the larger relational systems in which individuals are enmeshed. The study of internal group dynamics is only one aspect of structural configurations that may be meaningful for leisure behavior.

The structural approach presented in this book, in keeping with general orientations in traditional leisure research, highlights the importance of interpersonal relationships of sentiment and affection for leisure behaviors with family and friends. But are there other types of relationships through which enjoyment can be experienced in leisure contexts? Further, must leisure relationships always contain or produce only positive personal feelings? One can conceive of experiences that are not freely chosen (for example, attending a party because one feels one 'should'), or experiences that have less than ideal conditions for their duration (acts of nature, for instance, that adversely affect a hiking expedition). The context is still leisure, but the relationships may not be freely chosen or the resultant feelings necessarily positive. Structural analysis would allow researchers to explore the obligated, and perhaps unsatisfying, aspects of leisure experiences by considering the qualities and patterning of relational ties that constrain leisure behavior, and question whether and how negative experiences might affect future relational involvements.

Structural research in leisure must also be concerned with variations in relationships and structures over time, and with their influences on future leisure involvements. Often researchers consider only the activity participation stage of leisure, ignoring social antecedents and outcomes of leisure involvement. Theories that locate leisure contexts within broader social relationships of community provide the basis for considering changes in the composition, density, or partitioning of social networks over time. Research about life cycle stages is a partial effort at understanding time elements of leisure, but the idealized categories of life cycle research are not shared by all people, especially the disadvantaged or impoverished, the never married, or the 'new singles' who become widowed or divorced.

People make choices for involvement in social relationships, and then assume the consequences of involvement. A structural perspective suggests that consequences may not always be direct or limited: constraints or opportunities may be mediated by second- or third-order relationships beyond the immediate dyadic interaction. For example, invitations may be extended, but previous engagements might prevent participation. Families might hope to visit together at holidays, but external social demands on each participant may reduce time together. Moreover, network ties have 'latent' potential, and leisure involvement may not be an immediate outcome of new ties. Simply having 'enough' ties to others (whatever that amount may be) could be of equal value to actually activating those ties.

Likewise, gaining a friend or acquaintance means that one gains at least hypothetical access to that person's egocentric social network as well. The potential connectedness of multiple networks raises interesting questions about the ordering of social ties in leisure. For example, under what circumstances can associates in different parts of a person's network be brought together? And how strong does a relationship have to be between two people before each brings other close friends into a shared recreation event? What kinds of activity situations allow kin and friends to co-mingle? Finally, which specific network positions or linkages contain the most potential for creating, validating, or influencing leisure meanings?

One of the most interesting issues related to patterning of social relationships across networks in leisure contexts is that the largest proportion of ties in social networks seem to be weak ties. It could be hypothesized that there are a limited number of strong ties any social actor can maintain (the costs and benefits of involvement are limiting), so there will always be many more weak than strong ties across networks. Further, not all ties need to be activated at once. In fact, some will never be used, and others may produce few returns even if they are used. Given that the social ties activated for leisure have been assumed to be strong ties with close family and friends, one might speculate about the importance of weak ties in leisure networks. Are weak ties inconsequential, accumulating in rapid number only as a by-product of the development of strong ties? Or do weak ties have specific purpose and usefulness for leisure experiences?

Granovetter's (1973, 1982) research suggests that weak ties are useful for finding jobs and maintaining community cohesion, and Stokowski (1990b) found that weak ties provided general information for tourists. In addition, it may be hypothesized that weak ties, by serving as 'bridges' between strongly tied, cohesive network subgroups, provide pathways for diffusion of innovations, information, and meaning in leisure. That non-dense networks of recreationists at leisure places fail to function collectively is expected; the larger question is whether there are occasions when weak ties create opportunities for more organized, collective social behavior among previously unorganized participants.

Beyond their potential for stimulating social action, weak ties may also be valuable simply in reaffirming personal experience and confirming social reality across social networks. Having large, extended social networks of strong and weak ties may foster in social actors a sense of well-being, and also may be used by some social actors to signal or measure status. Being well-connected socially may have rewards (or threats) beyond the characteristics or numbers of specific others in the network.

In addition to analyzing the structuring of leisure relationships across social networks, researchers should also ask questions about the social mechanisms and interactions that produce alternative outcomes from similar beginnings in leisure contexts. For example, relationships and actions typical to leisure contexts do not always produce leisure experiences on the personal or small-group level, but can also result in collective behavior on a much larger scale. For example, voluntary association membership often arises from choices made to participate in good causes with friends, kin, or acquaintances during free time. Relationships typical to leisure contexts thus contribute to the development and persistence of affiliations that may result in nonleisure behaviors.

Many political, religious, environmental, and other social movements owe their memberships to relationships and activities initiated by people in leisure contexts. In fact, it may be proposed that leisure contexts provide the primary arena in which social movements and collective behaviors are initiated. While freedom of choice on a personal level may not translate into freedom of activity on a collective level (organizational goals may be focused and specific, and organizing processes may be more formalized), leisure contexts provide ingredients to support solidarity within social movements. The search for personal identity, the connections with close, intimate others, and the shared experiences of leisure contexts may do much to promote cohesion and confirm commitments within both socially desirable and, perhaps also, socially undesirable associations.

Beyond individual and collective experiences of leisure, the institutionalization of leisure across society should be addressed with structural research about corporate actors who produce, market, and organize leisure services. Analysis of exchange relationships may be valuable in understanding the relations between agencies and organizations involved in leisure provision. To what extent do agencies cooperate, or share resources and information, or define and work towards collective goals? How do patterns of interorganizational relations affect the leisure experiences of people?

Conclusions

The utility of a network structural perspective is in the effort to provide new orientations for understanding the social behaviors and meanings developed and reproduced in the context of leisure. The location of leisure within broad community networks of sentiment and belongingness extends earlier approaches that focused primarily on the bounded, social group involvements of leisure. The structural approach to leisure, however, considers the fluidity of relationships and networks in explaining variability in leisure behaviors and meanings. Social networks are not fixed in time or space but are the continually evolving arrangements and patterns of social relationships among systems of social actors. The influence of structuring processes on action, and the manipulation of structures by social actors, are the issues of interest in network structural analysis.

In leisure contexts, there are clearly sets of people who can be said to constitute 'social groups', but a structural perspective holds that these groups are simply strongly connected local clusters within extended networks of relationships. Limiting analysis to leisure groups ignores the structuring of relationships more broadly across society, and results in a sociology of leisure that misrepresents both the nature of relationships and the nature of social structures of leisure. Leisure is a social experience, not simply a personal or group activity.

How do individual actions and social structures reciprocally affect each other? This volume proposes that micro-level behaviors affect structural conditions in at least three ways: first, by acts of reproduction of structured social relationships and social meanings; second, by the collective influence of sheer numbers of reproduction; and third, by the density of behavioral reproductions across society. That is, leisure activities, relations, and meanings both replicate social structure and have potential to change social structure as a result of their presentation across social systems. Similarly, social structures influence action in several ways: first, by constraining free time or the conditions of engagement in leisure (by favoring other economic, political, geographic, or social conditions); second, by limiting opportunities across social networks; and third, by favoring strong ties over weak for leisure involvement. Each of these structural situations makes it difficult for individuals to make major revisions to institutionalized social systems and their corresponding structures.

The reproduction of leisure across society occurs at all levels of social organization. Individual behaviors and meanings are made social through group involvement with close, significant others, and through coexistence with others who generally behave in expected ways. Extended social communities, markets, organizations, and nations contribute to the institutionalization of leisure by reinforcing conditions, rules, and boundaries of acceptable leisure behaviors and choices. The social significance of leisure is in the patterning of relationships among all levels of formality and organization, and in the interactions between and across levels of order.

The structuring of leisure systems across society occurs within wider social and cultural arenas, so a sociology of leisure that focuses entirely on the unique qualities of leisure experience, independent of wider social life, is misleading. Leisure is not entirely separate or removed from other contexts of social action. A structural sociology of leisure must consider at least three important questions. First, to what extent do social relationships enacted in leisure contexts influence (or receive influence from) relationships in other contexts of social life (for example, work or community)? Second, to what extent does the reproduction of structure in leisure affect the structuring of relationships across entire social systems? And third, to what extent do social systems exert pressures on relationships and networks of leisure to maintain or change established patterns of behaviors or meanings?

While a structural sociology of leisure raises many new and interesting questions about leisure behavior, the practical relevance of this research is likely to remain in the context of community, where social positions are negotiated, information is transmitted, and social meanings are confirmed through involvement and interaction in both interpersonal and organizational relationships. Through community relationships, people obtain information about recreation opportunities, participate in social events with groups and sets of others, enjoy daily life and its sociable leisure moments, and discuss and support issues meaningful in their lives. Through community relationships, organizations cooperate and compete, influence publics with rhetoric, maintain linkages with key economic and political actors, and influence the lives of local residents. It is in the context of communities that relationships fail, that new linkages are formed, and that formal and informal ties persist over time and distance. The richness of community life provides for researchers the basic elements of a meaningful interpersonal and organizational structural sociology of leisure.

REFERENCES

Adams, R.G. (1987) Patterns of network change: a longitudinal study of friendships of elderly women. *The Gerontologist* **27** (2), 222-7.

Agar, M.H. (1986) *Speaking of Ethnography*. Beverly Hills, CA: Sage.

Alba, R.D. and Moore, G. (1978) Elite social circles. *Sociological Methods and Research* **7** (2), 167-88.

Alexander, J.C. and Giesen, B. (1987) From reduction to linkage: the long view of the micro-macro debate. In Alexander, J.C., Giesen, B., Munch, R., and Smelser, N.J. (eds.) *The Micro-Macro Link*. Berkeley, CA: University of California Press, 1-42.

Alexander, J.C., Giesen, B., Munch, R., and Smelser, N.J. (eds.) (1987) *The Micro-Macro Link*. Berkeley, CA: University of California Press.

Allen, R.H. (1980) Network analysis: a new tool for resource managers. In *Proceedings: 1980 National Outdoor Recreation Trends Symposium*. United States Department of Agriculture: General Technical Report NE-57, Northeastern Forest Experiment Station, United States Forest Service, 89-97.

Allison, M.T. (1988) Breaking boundaries and barriers: future directions in cross-cultural research. *Leisure Sciences* **10** (4), 247-59.

Allison, M.T. and Duncan, M.C. (1987) Women, work, and leisure: the days of our lives. *Leisure Sciences* **9** (3), 143-62.

Andrus, C. (1992) 'Friends' ensure memorable India stay. *Denver Post*, Sunday 21 June, 1, 8-9 (travel section).

Barnes, J.A. (1954) Class and communities in a Norwegian island parish. *Human Relations* **7**, 39-58.

Barnes, J.A. (1969) Graph theory and social networks: a technical comment on connectedness and connectivity. *Sociology* **3**, 215-32.

Barnes, J.A. (1972) *Social Networks*. Reading, MA: Addison-Wesley.

Baumgartner, R. and Heberlein, T.A. (1981) Process, goal, and social interaction in recreation: what makes an activity substitutable? *Leisure Sciences* **4** (4), 443-57.

Bender, T. (1978) *Community and Social Change in America*. Baltimore, MD: Johns Hopkins University Press.

Berger, B. (1962) The sociology of leisure: some suggestions. *Industrial Relations* **1** (February), 31-45.

Berger, P.L. and Kellner, H. (1964) Marriage and the construction of reality. *Diogenes* **46** (Summer), 1-24.

Berger, P.L. and Luckmann, T. (1966) *The Social Construction of Reality*. Garden City, NY: Doubleday & Co.

Berkowitz, S.D. (1982) *An Introduction to Structural Analysis: The Network Approach to Social Research*. Toronto: Butterworth & Co.

Berlinski, D. (1986) *Black Mischief: The Mechanics of Modern Science*. New York: William Morrow & Co.

Bernard, H.R., Killworth, P.D., and Sailer, L. (1980) Informant accuracy in social network data IV: a comparison of clique-level structure in behavioral and cognitive network data. *Social Networks* **2** (3), 191-218.

Blau, P.M. (ed.) (1975) *Approaches to the Study of Social Structure*. New York: Free Press.

Blau, P.M. (1981) Introduction: diverse views of social structure and their common denominator. In Blau, P.M. and Merton, R.K. (eds.) *Continuities in Structural Inquiry.* Beverly Hills, CA: Sage, 1–23.

Blau, P.M. (1982) Structural sociology and network analysis. In Marsden, P.V. and Lin, N. (eds.) *Social Structure and Network Analysis.* Beverly Hills, CA: Sage, 273–9.

Blumer, H. (1969) *Symbolic Interactionism: Perspective and Method.* Englewood Cliffs, NJ: Prentice-Hall.

Boissevain, J. (1974) *Friends of Friends: Networks, Manipulators, and Coalitions.* Oxford: Blackwell.

Bott, E. (1955) Urban families: conjugal roles and social networks. *Human Relations* 8, 345–84.

Bott, E. (1971) *Family and Social Network.* London: Tavistock.

Boulding, K.E. (1989) Social indicators of one-way transfers in organizations. In Anderson, J.A. (ed.) *Communication Yearbook 12.* Newbury Park: Sage, 670–4.

Breiger, R.L. (1974) The duality of persons and groups. *Social Forces* 53 (2), 181–90.

Brightbill, C.K. (1960) *The Challenge of Leisure.* Englewood Cliffs, NJ: Prentice-Hall.

Brockman, C.F. and Merriam, L.C., Jr. (1973) *Recreational Use of Wild Lands.* New York: McGraw-Hill.

Buber, M. (1965) *The Knowledge of Man: A Philosophy of the Interhuman.* (Trans. and ed. by M. Friedman.) New York: Harper & Row.

Buchanan, T., Christensen, J.E., and Burdge, R.J. (1981) Social groups and the meanings of outdoor recreation activities. *Journal of Leisure Research* 13 (3), 254–66.

Bultena, G.L. and Klessig, L.L. (1969) Satisfaction in camping: a conceptualization and guide to social research. *Journal of Leisure Research* 1 (4), 348–64.

Burch, W.R., Jr. (1969) The social circles of leisure: competing explanations. *Journal of Leisure Research* 1 (2), 125–47.

Burch, W.R., Jr. (1986) Ties that bind: the social benefits of recreation provision. In *A Literature Review, The President's Commission on Americans Outdoors.* Washington, DC: US Government Printing Office, 81–91 (values section).

Burdge, R.J. (1969) Levels of occupational prestige and leisure activity. *Journal of Leisure Research* 1 (3), 262–74.

Burdge, R.J. (1983) Making leisure and recreation research a scholarly topic: views of a journal editor, 1972–1982. *Leisure Sciences* 6 (1), 99–126.

Burdge, R.J. and Field, D.R. (1972) Methodological perspectives for the study of outdoor recreation. *Journal of Leisure Research* 4 (4), 63–72.

Burdge, R.J., Buchanan, T., and Christensen, J.E. (1981) A critical assessment of the state of outdoor recreation research. In Napier, T.L. (ed.) *Outdoor Recreation Planning, Perspectives, and Research.* Dubuque, IA: Kendall-Hunt, 3–11.

Burt, R.S. (1976) Positions in networks. *Social Forces* 55 (1), 93–122.

Burt, R.S. (1978) Cohesion versus structural equivalence as a basis for network subgroups. *Sociological Methods and Research* 7 (2), 189–212.

Burt, R.S. (1980) Models of network structure. *Annual Review of Sociology* 6, 79–141.

Burt, R.S. (1981) Studying status/role sets as ersatz network positions in mass surveys. *Sociological Methods and Research* 9 (3), 313–37.

Burt, R.S. (1987) A note on strangers, friends, and happiness. *Social Networks* 9 (4), 311–31.

Burt, R.S. and Minor, M.J. (eds.) (1983) *Applied Network Analysis: A Methodological Introduction.* Beverly Hills, CA: Sage.

Campbell, K.E., Marsden, P.V. and Hurlbert, J.S. (1986) Social resources and socioeconomic status. *Social Networks* 8 (1), 97–117.

Cheek, N.H., Jr. (1971) Toward a sociology of not-work. *Pacific Sociological Review* 14 (3), 245–58.

Cheek, N.H., Jr. (1976) Perspectives on the zoological park. In Cheek, N.H., Jr., Field, D.R., and Burdge, R.J. (eds.) *Leisure and Recreation Places.* Ann Arbor, MI: Ann Arbor, 47–57.

Cheek, N.H., Jr. and Burch, W.R., Jr, (1976) *The Social Organization of Leisure in Human Society.* New York: Harper & Row.

Cheek, N.H., Jr. and Field, D.R. (1977) Aquatic resources and recreation behavior. *Leisure Sciences* 1 (1), 67–83.

Cheek, NH., Jr., Field, D.R., and Burdge, R.J. (eds.) (1976) *Leisure and Recreation Places.* Ann Arbor, MI: Ann Arbor.

Christensen, J.E. (1980) Rethinking 'social groups as a basis for assessing participation in selected water activities.' *Journal of Leisure Research* 12 (4), 346–56.

Christensen, J.E. and Yoesting, D.R. (1973) Social and attitudinal variants in high and low use of outdoor recreation facilities. *Journal of Leisure Research* 5 (1), 6–15.

Clarke, A.C. (1956) The use of leisure and its relation to levels of occupational prestige. *American Sociological Review* 21 (3), 301–7.

Clawson, M. and Knetsch, J.L. (1966) *Economics of Outdoor Recreation.* Baltimore, MD: Johns Hopkins University Press.

Cobb, M. (1988) Influence and exchange networks among tourism oriented businesses in four Michigan communities. PhD thesis, Michigan State University, East Lansing, MI.

Cohen, A.P. (1985) *The Symbolic Construction of Community.* Chichester: Ellis Horwood.

Cohen, E. (1984) The sociology of tourism: approaches, issues, and findings. *Annual Review of Sociology* 10, 373–92.

Cohen-Mansfield, J. (1989) Employment and volunteering roles for the elderly: characteristics, attributions, and strategies. *Journal of Leisure Research* 21 (2), 214–27.

Coleman, J., Katz, E., and Menzel, H. (1957) The diffusion of an innovation among physicians. *Sociometry* 20, 253–70.

Coleman, J.S. (1975) Social structure and a theory of action. In Blau, P.M. (ed.) *Approaches to the Study of Social Structure.* New York: The Free Press, 76–93.

Colfer, C.J.P. with Colfer, A.M. (1978) Inside Bushler Bay: lifeways in counterpoint. *Rural Sociology* 43 (2), 204–20.

Collins, R. (1985) *Three Sociological Traditions.* New York: Oxford University Press.

Collins, R. (1987) Interaction ritual chains, power, and property: the micro–macro connection as an empirically-based theoretical problem. In Alexander, J.C., Giesen, B., Munch, R., and Smelser, N.J. (eds.) *The Micro–Macro Link.* Berkeley, CA: University of California Press, 193–206.

Colton, C.W. (1987) Leisure, recreation, and tourism: a symbolic interactionism view. *Annals of Tourism Research* 14, 345–60.

Conrath, D.W., Higgins C.A., and McClean, R.J. (1983) A comparison of the reliability of questionnaire versus diary data. *Social Networks* 5 (3), 315–22.

Coser, L.A., Nock, S.L., Steffan, P.A., and Rhea, B. (1987) *Introduction to Sociology*. New York: Harcourt Brace Jovanovich.

Crandall, R. (1979) Social interaction, affect, and leisure. *Journal of Leisure Research* 11 (3), 165–81.

Crompton, J.L. (1981) Dimensions of the social group role in pleasure vacations. *Annals of Tourism Research* 8 (4), 550–68.

Csikszentmihalyi, M. (1975) *Beyond Boredom and Anxiety*. San Francisco, CA: Jossey-Bass.

Csikszentmihalyi, M. (1990) *Flow: The Psychology of Optimal Experience*. New York: Harper & Row.

Dann, G. and Cohen, E. (1991) Sociology and tourism. *Annals of Tourism Research* 18, 155–69.

Davis, J.A. (1967) Clustering and balance in graphs. *Human Relations* 20, 181–7.

Dawson, D. (1984) Phenomenological approaches to leisure research. *Recreation Research Review* (1), 18–23.

Dawson, D. (1988) Social class in leisure: reproduction and resistance. *Leisure Sciences* 10 (3), 193–202.

de Grazia, S. (1962) *Of Time, Work, and Leisure*. Garden City, NY: The Twentieth Century Fund.

Department of Resource Development, Michigan State University (1962) *The Quality of Outdoor Recreation: As Evidenced by User Satisfaction*. Report to the Outdoor Recreation Resources Review Commission, No. 5. Washington, DC: Government Printing Office.

DeVall, B. (1976) Social worlds of leisure. In Cheek, N.H., Jr., Field, D.R., and Burdge, R.J. (eds.) *Leisure and Recreation Places*. Ann Arbor, MI: Ann Arbor, 131–42.

Ditton, R.B., Loomis, D.K., and Choi, S. (1992) Recreation specialization: re-conceptualization from a social worlds perspective. *Journal of Leisure Research* 24 (1), 33–51.

Doreian, P. (1986) On the evolution of group and network structure II: structures within structures. *Social Networks* 8 (1), 33–64.

Dottavio, F.D., O'Leary, J.T., and Koth, K. (1980) The social group variable in recreation participation studies. *Journal of Leisure Research* 12 (4), 357–67.

Driver, B.L., Brown, P.J., and Peterson, G.L. (eds.) (1991) *The Benefits of Leisure*. State College, PA: Venture Press.

Dumazdier, J. (1967) *Toward a Society of Leisure*. New York: Elsevier.

Eckstein, C.E. (1983) Communication networks of visitors to recreation locations along the Great Lakes: implications for increasing tourism. MS thesis, Michigan State University, East Lansing, MI.

The Ecologist (1992) The encompassing web: the ramifications of enclosure (editorial). *The Ecologist* 22 (4), 150–5.

Erickson, B.H. and Nosanchuk, T.A. (1983) Applied network sampling. *Social Networks* 5 (4), 367–82.

Erickson, B.H., Nosanchuk, T.A., and Lee, E. (1981) Network sampling in practice: some second steps. *Social Networks* 3 (2), 127–36.

Etzkorn, P.K. (1964) Leisure and camping: the social meaning of a form of public recreation. *Sociology and Social Research* 49, 76–89.

Field, D.R. and Cheek, N.H., Jr. (1974) A basis for assessing differential participation in water-based recreation. *Water Resources Bulletin* 10 (6), 1218–27.

Field, D.R. and Cheek, N.H., Jr. (1981) Focused and diffuse patterns of aquatic recreation behavior. *Water Resources Bulletin* 17 (1), 16–22.

Field, D.R. and O'Leary, J.T. (1973) Social groups as a basis for assessing participation in selected water activities. *Journal of Leisure Research* 5 (2), 16–25.

Filstead, W.J. (1976) Sociological paradigms of reality. In Garvin, H.R. (ed.) *Phenomenology, Structuralism, Semiology*. Lewisburg, PA: Bucknell University Press, 57–70.

Fischer, C.S. (1982a) What do we mean by 'friend'? An inductive study. *Social Networks* 3 (4), 287–306.

Fischer, C.S. (1982b) *To Dwell among Friends: Personal Networks in Town and City*. Chicago, IL: University of Chicago Press.

Fischer, C.S. and Phillips, S.L. (1979) *Who Is Alone? Social Characteristics of People with Small Networks*. Working Paper No. 310. Berkeley, CA: Institute of Urban and Regional Development, University of California.

Frank, L.K. et al. (1962) *Trends in American Living and Outdoor Recreation*. Report to the Outdoor Recreation Resources Review Commission, No. 22. Washington, DC: Government Printing Office.

Frank, O. (1978) Sampling and estimation in large social networks. *Social Networks* 1 (1), 91–101.

Freudenburg, W.R. (1986) The density of acquaintanceship: an overlooked variable in community research? *American Journal of Sociology* 92 (1), 27–63.

Friedkin, N. (1980) A test of structural features of Granovetter's strength of weak ties theory. *Social Networks* 2 (4), 411–22.

Galaskiewicz, J. (1979) *Exchange Networks and Community Politics*. Beverly Hills, CA: Sage.

Giddens, A. (1976) *New Rules of Sociological Method: A Positive Critique of Interpretative Sociologies*. New York: Basic Books.

Giddens, A. (1979) *Central Problems in Social Theory: Action, Structure, and Contradiction in Social Analysis*. Berkeley, CA: University of California Press.

Giddens, A. (1984) *The Constitution of Society: Outline of a Theory of Structuration*. Berkeley, CA: University of California Press.

Giddens, A. (1990) *The Consequences of Modernity*. Stanford, CA: Stanford University Press.

Gitelson, R.J. and Crompton, J.L. (1983) The planning horizons and sources of information used by pleasure vacationers. *Journal of Travel Research* 21 (3), 2–7.

Glancy, M. (1988) The play-world setting of the auction. *Journal of Leisure Research* 20 (2), 135–53.

Glancy, M. (1990) Socially-organized role-taking: becoming an auction player. *Leisure Sciences* 12 (4), 349–66.

Glaser, B. and Strauss, A. (1967) *The Discovery of Grounded Theory: Strategies for Qualitative Research*. New York: Aldine de Gruyter.

Glover, F. and Rogozinski, J. (1982) Resort development: a network-related model for optimizing sites and visits. *Journal of Leisure Research* 14 (3), 235–47.

Goodman, L. (1961) Snowball sampling. *Annals of Mathematical Statistics* 32, 148–70.

Graburn, N.H.H. (1989) Tourism: the sacred journey. In Smith, V.L. (ed.) *Hosts and Guests: The Anthropology of Tourism*. Philadelphia, PA: University of Pennsylvania Press, 21–36.

Granovetter, M. (1973) The strength of weak ties. *American Journal of Sociology* 78, (6), 1360–80.

Granovetter, M. (1976) Network sampling: some first steps. *American Journal of Sociology* 81 (6), 1287–303.

Granovetter, M. (1982) The strength of weak ties: a network theory revisited. In Marsden, P.V. and Lin, N. (eds.) *Social Structure and Network Analysis.* Beverly Hills, CA: Sage, 105–30.

Greenbaum, S.D. (1982) Bridging ties at the neighborhood level. *Social Networks* **4** (4), 367–84.

Greenblat, C.S. and Gagnon, J.H. (1983) Temporary strangers: travel and tourism from a sociological perspective. *Sociological Perspectives* **26**, 89–110.

Greenwood, D.J. (1989) Culture by the pound: an anthropological perspective on tourism as cultural commoditization. In Smith, V.L. (ed.) *Hosts and Guests: The Anthropology of Tourism.* Philadelphia, PA: University of Pennsylvania Press, 171–85.

Greenwood, J. (1992) Producer interest groups in tourism policy: case studies from Britain and the European Community. *American Behavioral Scientist* **36** (2), 236–56.

Guinn, R. (1980) Elderly recreational vehicle tourists: life satisfaction correlates of leisure satisfaction. *Journal of Leisure Research* **12** (3), 198–204.

Haggard, L.M. and Williams, D.R. (1992) Identity affirmation through leisure activities: leisure symbols of the self. *Journal of Leisure Research* **24** (1), 1–18.

Haines, V.A. (1988) Social network analysis, structuration theory, and the holism–individualism debate. *Social Networks* **10** (2), 157–82.

Hallinan, M.T. (1978) The process of friendship formation. *Social Networks* **1** (2), 193–210.

Hamilton, P. (1974) *Knowledge and Social Structure: An Introduction to the Classical Argument in the Sociology of Knowledge.* London: Routledge & Kegan Paul.

Hammer, M. (1984) Explorations into the meaning of social network interview data. *Social Networks* **6** (4), 341–71.

Hammer, M. (1985) Implications of behavioral and cognitive reciprocity in social network data. *Social Networks* **7** (2), 189–201.

Hantrais, L., Clark, P.A., and Samuel, N. (1984) Time–space dimensions of work, family, and leisure in France and Great Britain. *Leisure Studies* **3** (3), 301–17.

Harary, F. (1959/1977) Graph theoretic methods in the management sciences. In Leinhardt, S. (ed.) *Social Networks: A Developing Paradigm.* New York: Academic Press, 371–87.

Harary, F. and Batell, M.F. (1981) What is a system? *Social Networks* **3** (1), 29–40.

Harper, W. (1981) The experience of leisure. *Leisure Sciences* **4** (2), 113–26.

Harper, W. (1986) Freedom in the experience of leisure. *Leisure Sciences* **8** (2), 115–30.

Havitz, M.E. and Dimanche, F. (1990) Propositions for testing the involvement construct in recreational and tourism contexts. *Leisure Sciences* **12** (2), 179–95.

Heider, F. (1946/1977) Attitudes and cognitive organization. In Leinhardt, S. (ed.) *Social Networks: A Developing Paradigm.* New York: Academic Press, 3–8.

Hemingway, J.L. (1988) Leisure and civility: reflections on a Greek ideal. *Leisure Sciences* **10** (3), 179–91.

Hemingway, J.L. (1990) Opening windows on an [sic] interpretive leisure studies. *Journal of Leisure Research* **22** (4), 303–8.

Henderson, K.A. (1990) The meaning of leisure for women: an integrative review of research. *Journal of Leisure Research* **22** (3), 228–43.

Henderson, K.A. (1991a) The contributions of feminism to an understanding of leisure constraints. *Journal of Leisure Research* **23** (4), 363–77.

Henderson, K.A. (1991b) *Dimensions of Choice: A Qualitative Approach to Recreation, Parks, and Leisure Research.* State College, PA: Venture Press.

Henderson, K.A. and Rannells, J.S. (1988) Farm women and the meaning of work and leisure: an oral history perspective. *Leisure Sciences* 10 (1), 41–50.

Heywood, J.L. (1988) Leisure collectives: a theoretical perspective. *Leisure Sciences* 10 (2), 119–30.

Hoggett, P. and Bishop, J. (1985) Leisure beyond the individual consumer. *Leisure Studies* 4 (1), 21–38.

Holman, T.B. and Epperson, A. (1984) Family and leisure: a review of the literature with research recommendations. *Journal of Leisure Research* 16 (4), 277–94.

Homans, G.C. (1975) What do we mean by social 'structure'? In Blau, P.M. (ed.) *Approaches to the Study of Social Structure*. New York: Free Press, 53–65.

Horna, J.L.A. (1989) The leisure component of the parental role. *Journal of Leisure Research* 21 (2), 228–41.

Howe, C.Z. (1985) Possibilities for using a qualitative approach in the sociological study of leisure. *Journal of Leisure Research* 17 (3), 212–24.

Howe, C.Z. (1988) Using qualitative structured interviews in leisure research: illustrations from one case study. *Journal of Leisure Research* 20 (4), 305–23.

Huizinga, J. (1950) *Homo Ludens: A Study of the Play Element in Culture*. Boston, MA: Beacon Press.

Hull, R.B. (1990) Mood as a product of leisure: causes and consequences. *Journal of Leisure Research* 22 (2), 99–111.

Hutchison, R. (1988) A critique of race, ethnicity, and social class in recent leisure–recreation research. *Journal of Leisure Research* 20 (1), 10–30.

Irwin, P.N., Gartner, W.C., and Phelps, C.C. (1990) Mexican-American/Anglo cultural differences as recreation style determinants. *Leisure Sciences* 12 (4), 335–48.

Iso-Ahola, S.E. (1980) *The Social Psychology of Leisure and Recreation*. Dubuque, IA: Wm. C. Brown.

Iso-Ahola, S.E. and Weissinger, E. (1990) Perceptions of boredom in leisure: conceptualization, reliability, and validity of the leisure boredom scale. *Journal of Leisure Research* 22 (1), 1–17.

Jackson, E.L. (1991) Special issue introduction: leisure constraints/constrained leisure. *Leisure Sciences* 13 (4), 273–8.

Johnson, J.C. and Miller, M.L. (1983) Deviant social positions in small groups: the relation between role and individual. *Social Networks* 5 (1), 51–69.

Johnson, J.C. and Miller, M.L. (1986) Behavioral and cognitive data: a note on the multiplexity of network subgroups. *Social Networks* 8 (1), 65–77.

Jones, L.M. and Fischer, C.S. (1978) *Studying Egocentric Networks by Mass Survey*. Working Paper No. 284. Berkeley, CA: Institute of Urban and Regional Development, University of California.

Kando, T.M. (1975) *Leisure and Popular Culture in Transition*. St. Louis, MO: C.V. Mosby.

Kando, T.M. (1980) *Leisure and Popular Culture in Transition* (2nd edn.). St. Louis, MO: C.V. Mosby.

Kaplan, M. (1975) *Leisure: Theory and Policy*. New York: John Wiley & Sons.

Kelly, J.R. (1974) Socialization toward leisure: a developmental approach. *Journal of Leisure Research* 6 (2), 181–93.

Kelly, J.R. (1978) Family leisure in three communities. *Journal of Leisure Research* 10 (1), 47–60.

Kelly, J.R. (1982) *Leisure*. Englewood Cliffs, NJ: Prentice-Hall.

Kelly, J.R. (1983) *Leisure Identities and Interactions*. London: Allen & Unwin.

Kelly, J.R. (1986) Later life leisure: how they play in Peoria. *The Gerontologist* 26 (5), 531–7.

Kelly, J.R. (1992) Counterpoints in the sociology of leisure. *Leisure Sciences* 14 (3), 247–53.

Kelly, J.R. and Ross, J.E. (1989) Later-life leisure: beginning a new agenda. *Leisure Sciences* 11 (1), 47–59.

Kelly, J.R., Steinkamp, M.W., and Kelly, J.R. (1987) Later-life satisfaction: does leisure contribute? *Leisure Sciences* 9 (3), 189–200.

Kerr, W. (1962) *The Decline of Pleasure*. New York: Simon & Schuster.

Knoke, D. and Kuklinski, J.H. (1982) *Network Analysis*. Beverly Hills, CA: Sage.

Knopp, T.B. (1972) Environmental determinants of recreation behavior. *Journal of Leisure Research* 4 (2), 129–38.

Komarovsky, M. (1962) *Blue-Collar Marriage*. New York: Random House.

Kraus, R. (1971) *Recreation and Leisure in Modern Society*. New York: Meredith Corporation.

Kraus, R. (1984) *Recreation and Leisure in Modern Society* (3rd edn). Glenview, IL: Scott, Foresman & Co.

Larson, R.W. and Bradney, N. (1988) Precious moments with family members and friends. In Milardo, R.M. (ed.) *Families and Social Networks*. Newbury Park, CA: Sage, 107–26.

Lawton, M.P. and Moss, M. (1987) The social relationships of older people. In Borgatta, E.F. and Montgomery, R. (eds.) *Critical Issues in Aging Policy*. Beverly Hills, CA: Sage, 92–126.

Le Shan, L. and Margenau, H. (1982) *Einstein's Space and Van Gogh's Sky: Physical Reality and Beyond*. New York: Macmillan.

Lee, G.R. (1980) Kinship in the seventies: a decade review of research and theory. *Journal of Marriage and the Family* 42 (4), 923–34.

Lee, R.G. (1972) The social definition of outdoor recreational places. In Burch, W.R., Jr., Cheek, N.H., Jr., and Taylor, L. (eds.) *Social Behavior, Natural Resources, and the Environment*. New York: Harper & Row, 68–84.

Lee, R.G. (1977) Alone with others: the paradox of privacy in the wilderness. *Leisure Sciences* 1 (1), 3–19.

Leinhardt, S. (ed.) (1977) *Social Networks: A Developing Paradigm*. New York: Academic Press.

Levy, L. (1989) Community in a recreational setting. *Leisure Sciences* 11 (4), 303–22.

Lewis, E.R. (1977) *Network Models in Population Biology*. New York: Springer-Verlag.

Lin, N. (1982) Social resources and instrumental action. In Marsden, P.V. and Lin, N. (eds.) *Social Structure and Network Analysis*. Beverly Hills, CA: Sage, 131–45.

Lincoln, Y.S. and Guba, E.G. (1985) *Naturalistic Inquiry*. Beverly Hills, CA: Sage.

Linder, S.B. (1970) *The Harried Leisure Class*. New York: Columbia University Press.

Litwak, E. and Szelenyi, I. (1969) Primary group structures and their functions: kin, neighbors, and friends. *American Sociological Review* 34 (August), 465–81.

Lofland, J. and Lofland, L.H. (1984) *A Guide to Qualitative Observation and Analysis*. Belmont, CA: Wadsworth.

Lorrain, F. and White, H.C. (1971) Structural equivalence of individuals in social networks. *Journal of Mathematical Sociology* 1, 49–80.

Lucas, R.C. (1970) Wilderness perception and use: the example of the Boundary Waters Canoe Area. *Natural Resources Journal* 3 (3), 394–411.

Luckmann. T. (ed.) (1978) *Phenomenology and Sociology: Selected Readings*. New York: Penguin Books.

Lundberg, G.A., Komarovsky, M., and McInerny, M.A. (1934) *Leisure: A Suburban Study*. New York: Columbia University Press.

Lynd, R.S. and Lynd, H.M. (1929) *Middletown*. New York: Harcourt Brace.

Lynd, R.S. and Lynd, H.M. (1937) *Middletown in Transition: A Study in Cultural Conflicts*. New York: Harcourt Brace.

Lyon, L. (1987) *The Community in Urban Society*. Chicago, IL: Dorsey Press.

McAvoy, L.H. (1979) The leisure preferences, problems, and needs of the elderly. *Journal of Leisure Research* 11 (1), 40–47.

McCall, G.J. and Simmons, J.L. (eds.) (1978) *Identities and Interactions: An Examination of Human Associations in Everyday Life*. New York: Free Press.

McCall, G.J., McCall, M.M., Denzin, N.K., Suttles, G.D., and Kurth, S.B. (1970) *Social Relationships*. Chicago, IL: Aldine.

MacCannell, D. (1976) *The Tourist: A New Theory of the Leisure Class*. New York: Schocken Books.

McCool, S.F. (1978) Recreation activity packages at water-based resources. *Leisure Sciences* 1 (2), 163–73.

McCord, E. (1980) Structural-functionalism and the network idea: towards an integrated methodology. *Social Networks* 2 (4), 371–83.

McGoodwin, J.R. (1986) The tourism-impact syndrome in developing coastal communities: a Mexican case. *Coastal Zone Management Journal* 14, 131–46.

Macksey, R. and Donato, E. (eds.) (1972) *The Structuralist Controversy: The Languages of Criticism and the Sciences of Man*. Baltimore, PA: Johns Hopkins University Press.

Maines, D.R. (1977) Social organization and social structure in symbolic interactionist thought. *Annual Review of Sociology* 3, 235–59.

Mannell, R.C. and Iso-Ahola, S. (1985) Work constraints on leisure: a social psychological analysis. In Wade, M.G. (ed.) *Constraints on Leisure*. Springfield, IL: Charles C. Thomas, 155–87.

Mannell, R.C. and Stynes, D.J. (1991) A retrospective: the benefits of leisure. In Driver, B.L., Brown, P.J., and Peterson, G.L. (eds.) *The Benefits of Leisure*. State College, PA: Venture Press, 461–75.

Mannell, R.C. and Zuzanek, J. (1991) The nature and variability of leisure constraints in daily life: the case of the physically active leisure of older adults. *Leisure Sciences* 13, (4), 337–51.

Mannell, R.C., Zuzanek, J., and Larson, R. (1988) Leisure states and 'flow' experiences: testing perceived freedom and intrinsic motivation hypotheses. *Journal of Leisure Research* 20 (4), 289–304.

Manning, R.E. (1986) *Studies in Outdoor Recreation: A Review and Synthesis of the Social Science Literature in Outdoor Recreation*. Corvallis, OR: Oregon State University Press.

Marsden, P.V. and Lin, N. (eds.) (1982) *Social Structure and Network Analysis*. Beverly Hills, CA: Sage.

Matthews, S.H. (1986) *Friendships through the Life Course: Oral Biographies in Old Age*. Beverly Hills, CA: Sage.

Meyersohn, R. (1969) The sociology of leisure in the United States: introduction and bibliography, 1945–1965. *Journal of Leisure Research* 1 (1), 53–68.

Milardo, R.M. (1988a) Families and social networks: an overview of theory and methodology. In Milardo, R.M. (ed.) *Families and Social Networks*. Beverly Hills, CA: Sage, 13–47.

Milardo, R.M. (ed.) (1988b) *Families and Social Networks*. Beverly Hills, CA: Sage.

Milgram, S. (1967) The small world problem. *Psychology Today* 1 (May), 61–7.

Mitchell, J.C. (1969) The concept and use of social networks. In Mitchell, J.C. (ed.) *Social Networks in Urban Situations*. Manchester: Manchester University Press, 1–50.

Mitchell, J.C. (1987) The components of strong ties among homeless women. *Social Networks* 9 (1), 37–47.

Moody, H.R. (1986) The meaning of life and the meaning of old age. In Cole, T.R. and Gadow, S.A. (eds.) *What Does it Mean to Grow Old?* Durham, NC: Duke University Press, 9–40.

Moreno, J.L. (1934) *Who Shall Survive: A New Approach to the Problem of Human Interaction*. New York: Beacon House.

Moreno, J.L. (1951) *Sociometry, Experimental Method, and the Science of Society*. New York: Beacon House.

Mueller, E. and Gurin, G. (1962) *Participation in Outdoor Recreation: Factors Affecting Demand among American Adults*. Report to the Outdoor Recreation Resources Review Commission, No. 20. Washington, DC: Government Printing Office.

Munch, R. and Smelser, N.J. (1987) Relating the micro and macro. In Alexander J.C., Giesen, B., Munch, R., and Smelser, N.J. (eds.) *The Micro–Macro Link*. Berkeley, CA: University of California Press, 356–87.

Mundackal, J. (1977) *Man in Dialogue: A Study of Dialogue and Interpersonal Relationship According to Martin Buber*. Alwaye, Kerala, India: Little Flower Study House.

Murdock, S.H., Backman, K., Hoque, M.N., and Ellis, D. (1991) The implications of change in population size and composition on future participation in outdoor recreation activities. *Journal of Leisure Research* 23 (3), 238–59.

Nash, D. (1981) Tourism as an anthropological subject. *Current Anthropology* 22, 461–81.

Nash, D. and Smith, V.L. (1991) Anthropology and tourism. *Annals of Tourism Research* 18 (1), 12–25.

Neulinger, J. (1981) *The Psychology of Leisure*. Springfield, IL: Charles C. Thomas.

Newman, O. (1983) The coming of a leisure society? *Leisure Studies* 2 (1), 97–109.

Noe, F.P. (1970) A comparative typology of leisure in nonindustrialized society. *Journal of Leisure Research* 2 (1), 30–42.

Noe, F.P. (1992) Further questions about the measurement and conceptualization of backcountry encounter norms. *Journal of Leisure Research* 24 (1), 86–92.

O'Malley, M.E. (1984) Working with Sierra Leonean women in agriculture: an examination of conflicts and values. *Monterey Review* (Fall), 26–9.

Orthner, D.K. (1976) Patterns of leisure and marital interaction. *Journal of Leisure Research* 8 (1), 98–111.

Orthner, D.K. and Mancini, J.A. (1978) Parental family sociability and marital leisure patterns. *Leisure Sciences* 1 (4), 365–72.

Orthner, D.K. and Mancini, J.A. (1990) Leisure impacts on family interaction and cohesion. *Journal of Leisure Research* 22 (2), 125–37.

Parry, N.C.A. (1983) Sociological contributions to the study of leisure. *Leisure Studies* 2 (1), 57–81.

Pieper, J. (1952) *Leisure: The Basis of Culture*. (Trans. A. Dru). New York: Pantheon Books.

Pine, R. (1984) Community development and voluntary associations: case studies in Finland, England, and Ireland. *Leisure Studies* 3 (1), 107–21.

Price, F.V. (1981) Only connect? Issues in charting social networks. *Sociological Review* 29 (2), 283–312.

Radcliffe-Brown, A.R. (1940/1977) On social structure. In Leinhardt, S. (ed.) *Social Networks: A Developing Paradigm*. New York: Academic Press, 221–32.

Ragheb, M.G. and Griffeth, C.A. (1982) The contribution of leisure participation and leisure satisfaction to life satisfaction of older persons. *Journal of Leisure Research* 14 (4), 295–306.

Richards, E.F. (1980) Network ties, kin ties, and marital role organization: Bott's hypothesis reconsidered. *Journal of Comparative Family Studies* 11 (2), 139–51.

Richards, W.D. and Rice, R.E. (1981) The NEGOPY network analysis program. *Social Networks* 3 (3), 215–23.

Roberts, K. and Chambers, D.A. (1985) Changing 'times': hours of work/patterns of leisure. *World Leisure and Recreation* 27 (1), 17–23.

Robinson, J.P. (1977) *How Americans Use Time*. New York: Holt, Rinehart & Winston.

Rogers, E.M. (1987) Progress, problems, and prospects for network research: investigating relationships in the age of electronic communication technologies. *Social Networks* 9 (4), 285–310.

Rogers, E.M. and Kincaid, D.L. (1981) *Communication Networks: Toward a New Paradigm for Research*. New York: Free Press.

Roggenbuck, J.W., Williams, D.R., Bange, S.P., and Dean, D.J. (1991) River float trip encounter norms: questioning the use of the social norms concept. *Journal of Leisure Research* 23 (2), 133–53.

Rogler, L.H. and Procidano, M.E. (1986) The effect of social networks on marital roles: a test of the Bott hypothesis in an intergenerational context. *Journal of Marriage and the Family* 48 (4), 693–701.

Romney, A.K. and Weller, S.C. (1984) Predicting informant accuracy from patterns of recall among individuals. *Social Networks* 6 (1), 59–77.

Runger, C. and Wasserman, S. (1980) Longitudinal analysis of friendship formation. *Social Networks* 2, 143–54.

Rybczynski, W. (1991) *Waiting for the Weekend*. New York: Penguin Books.

Samdahl, D.M. (1988) A symbolic interactionist model of leisure: theory and empirical support. *Leisure Sciences* 10 (1), 27–39.

Samdahl, D.M. (1991) Issues in the measurement of leisure: a comparison of theoretical and connotative meanings. *Leisure Sciences* 13 (1), 33–49.

Samdahl, D.M. (1992) Leisure in our lives: exploring the common leisure occasion. *Journal of Leisure Research* 24 (1), 19–32.

Samdahl, D.M. and Kleiber, D.A. (1989) Self-awareness and leisure experience. *Leisure Sciences* 11, (1), 1–10.

Schwartz, H. and Jacobs, J. (1979) *Qualitative Sociology: A Method to the Madness*. New York: Free Press.

Scott, D. and Godbey, G.C. (1992) An analysis of adult play groups: social versus serious participation in contract bridge. *Leisure Sciences* 14 (1), 47–67.

Scott, D. and Willits, F.K. (1989) Adolescent and adult leisure patterns: a 37-year follow-up study. *Leisure Sciences* 11 (4), 323–35.

Searle, M.S. (1989) Testing the reciprocity norm in a recreation management setting. *Leisure Sciences* 11 (4), 353–65.

Searle, M.S. (1991) Propositions for testing social exchange theory in the context of ceasing leisure participation. *Leisure Sciences* 13 (4), 279–94.

Selin, S.W. and Beason, K. (1991) Interorganizational relations in tourism. *Annals of Tourism Research* 18 (4), 639–52.

Selin, S.W. and Howard, D.R. (1988) Ego involvement and leisure behavior: a conceptual specification. *Journal of Leisure Research* 20 (3), 237–44.

Shamir, B. (1992) Social correlates of leisure identity salience: three exploratory studies. *Journal of Leisure Research* **24** (4), 301–23.

Shaw, S.M. (1985a) The meaning of leisure in everyday life. *Leisure Sciences* **7** (1), 1–24.

Shaw, S.M. (1985b) Gender and leisure: inequalities in the distribution of leisure time. *Journal of Leisure Research* **17** (4), 266–82.

Shelby, B. (1981) Encounter norms in backcountry settings: studies of three rivers. *Journal of Leisure Research* **13** (2), 129–38.

Shibutani, T. (1986) *Social Processes: An Introduction to Sociology*. Berkeley, CA: University of California Press.

Simmel, G. (1950) *The Sociology of Georg Simmel*. (Trans. and ed. K.A. Wolff.) New York: Free Press.

Smith, C.W. (1979) *A Critique of Sociological Reasoning: An Essay in Philosophical Sociology*. Oxford: Blackwell.

Smith, M.A. (1985) A participant observation study of a 'rough' working-class pub. *Leisure Studies* **4** (3), 293–306.

Smith, S. (1975) Towards meta-recreation research. *Journal of Leisure Research* **7** (3), 236–7.

Smith, V.L. (1989) *Hosts and Guests: The Anthropology of Tourism*. Philadelphia, PA: University of Pennsylvania Press.

Steene, A. (1991) Personal network as a business strategy. *Annals of Tourism Research* **18** (4), 666–8.

Steuve, A. and Fischer, C.S. (1978) *Social Networks and Older Women*. Working Paper No. 292. Berkeley, CA: Institute of Urban and Regional Development, University of California.

Stewart, D. and Mickunas, A. (1974) *Exploring Phenomenology*. Chicago, IL: American Library Association.

Stokowski, P.A. (1988) A revised sociology of leisure: the social relationships and network structures of leisure behaviors. PhD dissertation, University of Washington, Seattle, WA.

Stokowski, P.A. (1990a) Extending the social groups model: social network analysis in recreation research. *Leisure Sciences* **12** (3), 251–63.

Stokowski P.A. (1990b) Exploring the meaning of strong vs. weak social network ties. In *Abstracts of the Proceedings of the 1990 National Recreation and Parks Association Leisure Research Symposium*. Alexandria, VA: National Recreation and Parks Association.

Stokowski, P.A. (1992) Social networks and tourist behavior. *American Behavioral Scientist* **36** (2), 212–21.

Stokowski, P.A. and Lee, R.G. (1991) The influence of social network ties on recreation and leisure: an exploratory study. *Journal of Leisure Research* **23** (2), 95–113.

Stokowski, P.A., Long, P.T., and Nuckolls, J.S. (1992) Recreation leadership as a system of social ties. *Journal of Park and Recreation Administration* **10** (2), 67–77.

Sudman, S. (1985) Experiments in the measurement of the size of social networks. *Social Networks* **7** (2), 127–51.

Szalai, A. et al. (1972) *The Uses of Time: Daily Activities of Urban and Suburban Populations in 12 Countries*. The Hague: Mouton.

Theunissen, M. (1986) *The Other: Studies in the Social Ontology of Husserl, Heidegger, Sartre, and Buber* (trans. C. Macann). Cambridge, MA: MIT Press.

Tichy, N.M., Tushman, M.L., and Fombrun, C. (1979) Social network analysis for organizations. *Academy of Management Review* **4** (4), 507–19.

Tiryakian, E.A. (1970) Structural sociology. In McKinney, J.C. and Tiryakian, E.A. (eds.) *Theoretical Sociology: Perspectives and Developments*. New York: Meredith Corporation, 111–35.

Travers, J. and Milgram, S. (1969) An experimental study of the small world problem. *Sociometry* **32**, 425–43.

Turner, C. (1967) Conjugal roles and social networks: a re-examination of an hypothesis. *Human Relations* **20**, 121–30.

Turner, J.H. (1982) *The Structure of Sociological Theory*. Homewood, IL: Dorsey Press.

Udry, J.R. and Hall, M. (1965) Marital role segregation and social networks in middle-class middle-aged couples. *Journal of Marriage and the Family* **27** (3), 392–5.

Unruh, D.R. (1979) Characteristics and types of participation in social worlds. *Symbolic Interaction* **2**, 115–29.

van Ghent, D. and Brown, J. (eds.) (1968) *Continental Literature: An Anthology*. Vol. 1. New York: J.B. Lippincott.

van Poucke, W. (1980) Network constraints on social action: preliminaries for a network theory. *Social Networks* **2** (2), 181–90.

Veblen, T. (1899) *The Theory of the Leisure Class: An Economic Study of Institutions*. New York: Macmillan.

von Bertalanffy, L. (1950) The theory of open systems in physics and biology. *Science* **111**, 23–8.

Wagner, H.R. (ed.) (1970) *On Phenomenology and Social Relations: Selected Writings of Alfred Schutz*. Chicago, IL: University of Chicago Press.

Walter, J.A. (1984) Death as recreation: armchair mountaineering. *Leisure Studies* **3** (1), 67–76.

Warnick, B. (1979) Structuralism vs. phenomenology: implications for rhetorical criticism. *The Quarterly Journal of Speech* **65**, 250–61.

Warren, R.L. and Lyon, L. (eds.) (1988) *New Perspectives on the American Community*. Chicago, IL: Dorsey Press.

Wellman, B. (1979) The community question: the intimate networks of East Yorkers. *American Journal of Sociology* **84** (5), 1201–31.

Wellman, B. (1988) Structural analysis: from method and metaphor to theory and substance. In Wellman, B. and Berkowitz, S.D. (eds.) *Social Structures: A Network Approach*. Cambridge: Cambridge University Press, 19–61.

Wellman, B. and Berkowitz, S.D. (1988a) Introduction: studying social structures. In Wellman, B. and Berkowitz, S.D. (eds.) *Social Structures: A Network Approach*. Cambridge: Cambridge University Press, 1–14.

Wellman, B. and Berkowitz, S.D. (eds.) (1988b) *Social Structures: A Network Approach*. Cambridge: Cambridge University Press.

West, P.C. (1982) A nationwide test of the status group dynamics approach to outdoor recreation demand. *Leisure Sciences* **5** (1), 1–18.

West, P.C. (1984) Status differences and interpersonal influence in the adoption of outdoor recreation activities. *Journal of Leisure Research* **16** (4), 350–4.

West, P.C. and Merriam, L.C., Jr. (1970) Outdoor recreation and family cohesiveness: a research approach. *Journal of Leisure Research* **2** (4), 251–9.

White, H.C. (1988) Varieties of markets. In Wellman, B. and Berkowitz, S.D. (eds.) *Social Structures: A Network Approach*. Cambridge: Cambridge University Press, 226–60.

Whittaker, D. and Shelby, B. (1988) Types of norms for recreation impacts: extending the social norms concept. *Journal of Leisure Research* **20** (4), 261–73.

Williams, A.M. and Shaw, G. (1992) Tourism research: a perspective. *American Behavioral Scientist* **36** (2), 133–43.

Williams, D.R., Patterson, M.E., Roggenbuck, J.W., and Watson, A.E. (1992) Beyond the commodity metaphor: examining emotional and symbolic attachment to place. *Leisure Sciences* **14** (1), 29–46.

Wilson, J. (1980) Sociology of leisure. *Annual Review of Sociology* **6**, 21–40.

Wilson, R.N. (1981) The courage to be leisured. *Social Forces* **60** (2), 282–303.

Wilson, T.P. (1982) Relational networks: an extension of sociometric concepts. *Social Networks* **4** (2), 105–16.

Woodard, M.D. (1988) Class, regionality, and leisure among urban Black Americans: the post-civil rights era. *Journal of Leisure Research* **20** (2), 87–105.

Wuthnow, R., Hunter, J.D., Bergesen, A., and Kurzweil, E. (1984) *Cultural Analysis: The Work of Peter L. Berger, Mary Douglas, Michel Foucault, and Jürgen Habermas*. London: Routledge & Kegan Paul.

Yi, E.K. (1986) Implications of conjugal role segregation for extrafamilial relationships: a network model. *Social Networks* **8** (2), 119–47.

Yoesting, D.R. and Christensen, J.E. (1978) Re-examining the significance of childhood recreation on adult leisure behavior. *Leisure Sciences* **1** (3), 219–30.

Index

Index

Clarke, A.C. 18
class, social 4, 13, 17–20
Clawson, M. 5, 18, 87
Cobb, M. 75
Cohen, A.P. 49
Cohen, E. 50
Cohen-Mansfield, J. 25
Coleman, J.S. 44, 59
Colfer, A.M. 68
Colfer, C.J.P. 68
collectives, leisure 34
Collins, R. 32, 42
Colton, C.W. 32
common leisure occasions 34
community
  defined 49
  and leisure 13, 105, 117
  networks 48–51, 67–8, 74–5, 76–85,
    90–3
  personal communities 15, 16
  timber-dependent 76–85
Conrath, D.W. 69
context 30–1, 34–5, 37–8, 50, 88,
    101–2, 105, 113, 117
Coser, L.A. 40
Crandall, R. 13
Crompton, J.L. 23, 74
Csikszentmihalyi, M. 4
culture 14, 23

daily life 2, 33–5, 37, 73
Dann, G. 50
Davis, J.A. 58
Dawson, D. 18, 33
de Grazia, S. 4
density 89
Department of Resource Development,
    Michigan State University 20
De Vall, B. 35
Dimanche, F. 19
Ditton, R.B. 34
Donato, E. 39, 98

Doriean, P. 60
Dottavio, F.D. 22
Driver, B.L. 94
Dumazdier, J. 4
Duncan, M.C. 33

Eatonville 76–85, 88–90, 98
  leisure meanings 98–9
  leisure styles 79
  participation types 80
  recreation choices 80–2
  social relationships 78–9
  spousal networks 82–4
  structural patterns 80–1
Eckstein, C.E. 74
Ecologist, The 1
egocentric networks 59, 73
environment, social 112–14
Epperson, A. 24
Erickson, B.H. 70
ethnicity 19–20
Etzkorn, P.K. 20–1
exchange relations 45, 46, 68, 92
exchange theory 33, 69, 85–6

family
  aging 25
  cohesiveness 24
  conjugal roles 23–5, 67–8
  interaction patterns 24–5
  learning 24
  life cycle 23–6
  personal communities 24
  social roles 24
feminism 33
Field, D.R. 20, 21, 22
Filstead, W.J. 33, 96
Fischer, C.S. 59, 60, 62, 67, 68, 70,
    72, 77
flow 4
Frank, L.K. 15

and relationships 43
  social 39–42, 54
structuration
  action 101
  institutions 102–4
  and leisure 104–6
  meaning 103–4
  modernity 105
  structure 102
  theory 100–6
  time and space 101, 103
Stynes, D.J. 94, 110
Sudman, S. 69
symbolic interactionism 32, 34, 36
Szalai, A. 6
Szelenyi, I. 68

Theunissen, M. 44
Tichy, N.M. 58, 67
ties, social, *see* relationships
time
  and context 38
  free time 2, 5–7, 36
  leisure as 5–7
  time budget studies 6
  time-space relations 103, 105
Tiryakian, E.A. 40
tourism
  agencies 50–1
  authenticity 32
  communities 23
  hosts–guests 23, 92
  networks 50, 71–2, 74–5, 86, 92–3
  rituals 23
  travel groups 23
Travers, J. 59, 69
Turner, C. 68
Turner, J.H. 12, 32, 33, 39, 63, 95

Udry, J.R. 68

Unruh, D.R. 34

van Ghent, D. 5
van Poucke, W. 70
Veblen, T. 13, 18
voluntary associations 34
von Bertalanffy, L. 58

Wagner, H.R. 33, 95, 96
Walter, J.A. 35
Warnick, B. 98
Warren, R.L. 49
Wasserman, S. 68
weak ties 69, 74–5, 89, 115
  and strong ties 78
Weissinger, E. 19
Weller, S.C. 69
Wellman, B. 39, 41, 44, 55, 56, 57, 59,
  60, 67, 68, 69, 77
West, P.C. 19, 24
White, H.C. 58, 85
Whittaker, D. 36
Williams, A.M. 92–3
Williams, D.R. 36
Willits, F.K. 24
Wilson, J. 7
Wilson, R.N. 4
Wilson, T.P. 70
Woodard, M.D. 19
work 6–7, 14, 18
Wuthnow, R. 98

Yi, E.K. 68
Yoesting, D.R. 24

Zuzanek, J. 25